"I don't know a person who hasn't missed some red flags when it comes to relationships. So often the hope and excitement of a new relationship leads us to see what we want to see instead of seeing what is really there. I have listened to countless people with broken hearts because they missed the red flags that were clearly there. Learning how to recognize the good and bad signs of any potential relationship is a critical step towards health and wholeness. Dr. Conway Edwards provides incredible wisdom and time tested truths in this book that will help every reader navigate relationships with purpose instead of pain. This is a must read!"

Van Moody, Bestselling Author of *The People Factor*, *The I Factor* & *Desired By God*

"Watch the Flags is a game-changer for anyone navigating through today's complicated dating scene. Conway's ability to break down practical ways to spot both good and bad indicators in a potential relationship is exactly what reader's need. It's a GPS for relationships. If you're single you absolutely need this!"

Dr. Dharius Daniels, Author and Lead Pastor of Change Church

In a culture where toxic relationships are the "norm", Conway has taken on the challenge to lead Christians in establishing a healthy "norm" for relationships. Watch The Flags is a progressive blueprint for singles to discern the relational warning signs (flags) that are present, but often ignored when dating. Not only are readers challenged to identify the flags in others, but more importantly, they are challenged to be self-aware and identify flags within themselves. This book is a necessary tool needed to pursue healthy, God-honoring relationships.

Jada Edwards, Bible Teacher and Author

© 2022

Dr. Conway Edwards
Watch The Flags

All rights reserved. No part of this publication may be reproduced, stored in a retrieval system or transmitted in any form or by any means, electronic, mechanical, photocopying, recording or otherwise without the prior permission of the publisher or in accordance with the provisions of the Copyright, Designs and Patents Act 1988 or under the terms of any licence permitting limited copying issued by the Copyright Licensing Agency.

A CIP record for this book is available from the Library of Congress Cataloging-in-Publication Data

ISBN-13: 979-8-218-06140-1

WATCH THE FLAGS

Discerning Relational Signs in Dating

TABLE OF CONTENTS

INTRODUCTION 7

CHAPTER ONE
CHARACTER FLAGS 13

CHAPTER TWO
EXPECTATION FLAGS 25

INTERLUDE
THE FIVE BUCKETS 33

CHAPTER THREE
RELATIONAL FLAGS 41

CHAPTER FOUR
EMOTIONAL FLAGS 51

CHAPTER FIVE
SEXUAL FLAGS 61

CHAPTER SIX
SPIRITUAL FLAGS 73

CHAPTER SEVEN
PERSONAL GROWTH FLAGS 85

CHAPTER EIGHT
SOCIAL FLAGS 95

CHAPTER NINE
CONFLICT FLAGS 105

CONCLUSION 117

INTRODUCTION

Have you ever watched people do something painful to themselves? Sure, we all have. Maybe it was an athlete in a game or one of those "fail" videos. There is no shortage of opportunities to witness self-inflicted damage. Gus Frerotte is one example. He was the quarterback for the Washington Redskins in 1997 when, following a touchdown, his endzone celebration involved headbutting the wall. It didn't end well. Frerotte had to leave the game for a sprained neck. That's self-inflicted damage.

Seeing people you don't know unintentionally hurt themselves is one thing; when you know the person, however, it becomes much harder to bear watching the pain. This pain is rarely physical but is often the personal turmoil that comes from poor choices. A poor choice doesn't usually exist in isolation; it comes with several poor choices, each contributing to a little more pain and misery.

Maybe you have been there. It could be that your financial spending has gotten out of control and led to debt or the inability to cover important costs. Or perhaps personal habits have kept you from consistency on the job – even costing you your job. Relationships might have been strained by a quick temper or poorly-kept commitments. We have all learned the hard way about the pain that comes from poor choices.

Experience teaches maturity, and you have surely learned a life lesson or two. Those lessons build wisdom so that the next time you are faced with a similar choice, you can avoid the option that will cause sorrow and regret. Whether it's learning to eat out less to ensure you have enough gas money, getting a decent night's sleep to ensure you make it to work on time the next day, or finding ways to keep your cool when you are annoyed, wisdom helps you avoid the unpleasant results of unwise choices.

Yet not all learn from experience. Some people make the same mistakes over and over and cannot seem to connect the dots between their choices and the results that come from them. The cause and effect are lost on them, or they are dimly aware of it but still make the same foolish choices, hoping that the results will magically be different this time. Those doing the same thing while hoping for different results are perhaps the hardest to watch make choices that cause self-inflicted damage. Somehow, it's more tragic when their pain does not lead to maturity.

The Bible mentions this very phenomenon, where some develop wisdom about their choices while others do not. In Proverbs, it says, "A prudent man sees evil and hides himself, the naive proceed and pay the penalty."[1] Those who are wise – prudent – look ahead and recognize that they are about to make a choice that will lead to danger. They respond by choosing a safe alternative. The naïve, however, do not recognize the warning signs, so they keep going. They plunge ahead heedless of danger. That's not bravery. It's foolishness, and it costs them dearly!

> *"A whole heap of unwise choices has caused a lot of heartaches, heartbreak, and heartburn."*

Avoiding danger and heartache does not have to come from learning the hard way. Plenty of people have made foolish choices before you, leaving an example of what *not* to follow. Others have chosen wisely and revealed the conditions for living life to the fullest and minimizing the heartache of unwise choices.

That's where romantic relationships come into play. A whole heap of unwise choices has caused a lot of heartaches, heartbreak, and heartburn. The dating scene is littered with casualties, as immature people hook up and blow up. They come with issues, and a relationship only makes those issues worse.

Somebody should warn others so they can avoid the troubles that so often come with relationships.

That's what this book is about – Flags.

THE FLAGS

Have you ever spent a day at the beach? If you have, you may have noticed the flags that are set up in different areas. The flags indicate the condition of the water. When you see green flags, you have a great place to swim. It means someone

---
[1] Proverbs 27:12, NASB95

had gone before you and looked at the currents in the water. That person has determined those conditions to be safe. Green flags are good. You also have probably seen red flags. Those flags state that it is not safe to swim. Someone has gone before you, seen the conditions of the water, and determined that swimming is not a good idea.

Green flags indicate it is safe to proceed. Red flags warn against moving further.

These flags exist in the realm of dating. You'll find green and red flags in this book.

Someone has gone ahead of you. There are certain conditions in the world of dating that indicate it is either safe to proceed or unsafe. This is based on the experiences of others who have been in similar circumstances. The red flags indicate it is unsafe to proceed. If you do, you will likely inflict pain and heartache upon yourself. The green flags indicate it is safe to proceed. If the conditions are right, you will enjoy a good relationship with your boyfriend or girlfriend, who might one day become your husband or wife.

In the pages ahead, you'll find thirteen green flags and ten red flags that will help you know how to proceed in the most important of human relationships: the one that could lead to a lifelong marriage commitment.

The flags are divided into various categories to help you consider those areas as they relate to relationships. You might wish to jump to chapters that pique your interest first before getting to the others. That's okay.

But the thing about the flags is that once you know about them, you are responsible for them. Once you know something, you hold the burden of acting upon that knowledge. Some people do not want that kind of responsibility.

So be careful.

If you would like to know more about the flags – if you are ready for that responsibility – then read on.

CHAPTER ONE

CHARACTER FLAGS

Most people want to date a person with good character. What is character? It is what flows from a person's values and convictions. Character is formed on the inside and produced on the outside. If you find a guy who believes a woman's needs come second to the man's and thinks she exists only to serve him, you won't like his character. If you date a woman whose opinions are so fluid that she bases her beliefs on yours, it may seem nice, but without deep character, you will struggle to ever gain that soul-to-soul connection you long for. Character bubbles up to the surface and reveals what a person really believes.

So, what are the character flags to watch out for?

🚩 **Red Flag**: When their character is not what attracts you to them

> *"Finding out about a person's character is less like a deep-down mining expedition and more like collecting seashells."*

If character matters are not at the top of your list, look out! Oh, our hearts will throb with attraction for many superficial reasons: curves, clothes, cars, or crypto. People often dwell on surface-level traits, but character is where the substance of connection is found.

Ladies, a guy will come along and seem like the total package. He's 6'2", athletic, doesn't live in his mom's basement, and has a real job! But if you notice that he doesn't respect others, what do you think he's going to do to you once he thinks he has you? When he stops trying to impress you, you will be treated the way he treats everyone else. His casual lying to his parents or boss might seem like a funny way to fudge the truth right now, but what happens when he's explaining why he's out late for the third night this week? His character will have been the same as when you started dating him; it's just that the most appealing aspects are directed more toward you now.

However, we provide cover and say, "He's a good person *deep down*." A person will make excuses for a boyfriend or girlfriend just to stay in a relationship and not face the fact that there are BIG character flaws. What does this *deep-down* argument even mean? It means there are obvious problems on the surface that everyone can see – the red flag is waving prominently from all angles – but you ignore all of that and claim that your boo is a diamond in the rough. Finding out about a person's character is less like a deep-down mining expedition and more like collecting seashells. Couples need to probe the depths of each other's souls to determine some pretty important heart matters, dreams, and passions. You don't want a close-up view of her character by donning a hard hat and going down a long shaft to a series of tunnels, braving cave-ins and unbreathable conditions to find a worthwhile nugget. You should be able to stroll along and see good character in her. The undulating waves and current of her life continually wash in the evidence that she is an upright woman of high moral standing.

Ruth was known for her good character, and Boaz's heart went pitter patter because of it. He said, "Now, my daughter, do not fear. I will do for you whatever you ask, for all my people in the city know that you are a woman of excellence."[1] Ruth was known for being loyal, caring for her mother-in-law, and not engaging in mindless chatter but instead remaining dedicated to her work. Then she approached Boaz and asked him to redeem her family by taking her as his wife. Notice what Boaz didn't say his reasons were for agreeing. He didn't say he would do it because, "You're curvy in all the right places," or, "Imagine what those city elders will say when they see me riding up with you on my arm."

The problem with being attracted by traits other than character is that those other traits don't last. Curves become wrinkled, lumpy, and saggy. Fortunes reverse, leaving the wealthy penniless. Jobs are lost. Status can change quickly. What will you be attracted to when the thing that attracted you is gone? What do you do when the bottom drops out and takes your relationship with it? If it isn't character that attracts you, then relational struggle is on the horizon. You may hope it will last forever, but it won't.

---

1   Ruth 3:11, NASB95

What sort of good character should you look for? Wouldn't it be nice if there were some sort of list of traits that promote stable relationships – a master list that tells you what to seek?

There is!

> **Green Flag: You both exhibit the Fruit of the Spirit**

Fruit is one of the great gifts we get to enjoy on earth. Maybe you enjoy a juicy mango, a ripe peach, a crisp apple, or a pear whose juices dribble down your chin. Fruit is delicious. It tantalizes our tastebuds with incredible bursts of sugary flavor. All the energy in a plant is directed toward producing that delicious fruit. A couple whose energies are devoted to producing fruit is just as sweet.

Remember, character is formed on the inside and produced on the outside. Countless varieties of trees and vines exist, but only a few types are known for producing amazing fruit. You can find someone to date you, but a person of fruit-producing character is uncommon.

What list of character traits should you look for? The Bible holds the answer in the book of Galatians:

> *"But the fruit of the Spirit is love, joy, peace, patience, kindness, goodness, faithfulness, gentleness, self-control; against such things, there is no law."*[2]

These nine traits are collectively called "the fruit of the Spirit." It's your character scorecard. God knew you would need a list and gave you one, but here's the odd thing: People make up their own lists. People look at physical attributes, facial symmetry, fashion sense, height, weight, orthodontal

---
2   Galatians 5:22-23, NIV

history, influence, charisma, career path, Instagram followers, and a zillion other external features to determine their soulmates. We have inverted our priorities so that character takes a backseat to all sorts of less important characteristics.

The fruit of the Spirit is the foundation for a solid relationship, the sure way to reorder priorities.

LOVE

No, not that kind of love. This is not about whether the romance is there. It's about whether you can see evidence of a loving spirit that seeks the welfare of others at one's own expense. Does she visit her grandmother and help her clean? Does he take time for his little sister? His mother? Outside the family, do you notice a concern for the well-being of friends or even coworkers? Not having such love will lead to a callous disregard for others. If they do not show concern for people in their lives, you will one day be one of those people. In the short term, the flames of passion put you in a special category, but they will die down soon enough. Make sure the right kind of love is there from the start.

JOY

Being around joyful people makes you joyful, too. You become excited just by being around them! Wouldn't it be nice to date a joyful person, too? Joy has been defined as the "experience of great pleasure or delight." Though often described as an emotion, joy is more a positive attitude that a person decides to have, based on unchanging conditions. Many people confuse joy with happiness, but happiness is based on changing conditions.

For example, the emotions that children show are often based on changing conditions. If you tell a child he is getting a

> "Being a person of peace means you don't feed on drama but are more likely to overlook an offense."

popsicle, he's happy. Oops, we're out of the red ones. Now he's sad. We're going to the playground – happy! Uh oh. An unexpected storm is rolling in – sad. If you do one fun thing, like playing a board game or renting a movie, you might hear, "This is the best day ever!" Kids exhibit happiness, which is simply a response to external stimuli. That's not much different from the reflex test the doctor gives by tapping that little rubber mallet on your knee.

Joy is not a reflex. Joy is a mature response a person develops despite external conditions. It comes from gratitude and an assurance that a loving God is in control of the past, present, and future. These unchanging conditions allow him to have a bad day and still stay positive rather than have a melt down. It enables her to lose out on a promotion yet still be content in her day-to-day life. This does not mean someone is giddy and gleeful when terrible things happen. Run from a person like that because you're dating a circus clown who has no off switch. Find someone with true joy, however, and you'll have someone to navigate life with while staying positive.

PEACE

We all want world peace, and personal relationships are a great place to start. Have you ever seen a couple whose relationship seems to consist of one endless stream of conflicts? Some are big, some are small, but those conflicts dominate their lives. Maybe you have been there, too. Being a person of peace means you don't feed on drama but are more likely to overlook an offense. To show peace requires first having peace – an inner equilibrium – that can avoid overreacting to situations.

Were you ever afraid of the bogeyman? Any little noise or shadow in your room sent you running for Mom! Adults without peace are set off by little facial expressions, offhanded comments, or imagined intentions. It's not a good way to live, and it's certainly not a good basis for a relationship. Find a person who exhibits peace if you want a relationship without unnecessary drama.

PATIENCE

This one is sometimes called forbearance, which is the art of putting up with people. A young wife discovered her husband's impatience when her car broke down, and, stranded on the roadside, she called him to ask for help. Unfortunately, he was in the middle of watching his favorite NFL team play. He begrudgingly went to pick her up but not without lecturing her and demanding that next time, if it's during a game, she should call someone else. Do you think that marriage lasted?

Patience isn't just for unforeseen emergencies; it's also for our idiosyncrasies, those weird little oddities of our behavior. Let's face the fact that putting up with you won't be a picnic! Couples who practice patience will, without complaint, put up with laundry on the floor, toilet seats raised or lowered, dirty dishes left out, having to work late, in-laws, bad days, muttering, sarcasm, and unfinished projects. That's really what we all are – unfinished projects which require patience from those closest to us, the same patience our loving God has for us. A person with patience will not complain about every little issue but will instead practice the art of putting up with you as you grow and mature.

KINDNESS AND GOODNESS

If goodness is the root, kindness is the fruit. When you're a hot mess, you need more than patience; you need a person to express kindness to you. In Proverbs, it states, "A gentle answer turns away wrath, but a harsh word stirs up anger."[3] Kindness – that expression of goodness – can dial down a situation before it escalates and bring positivity. What fuels kindness? We are told in the Bible, "Be kind to one another, tender-hearted, forgiving each other, just as God in Christ also has forgiven you."[4] The kindness received – forgiveness of our own sins by Jesus – is a source of internalized goodness that then begets kindness.

In other words, the recipient of kindness finds his character changed and improved, developing goodness within him through the prompting of the Holy Spirit. That goodness then spills out into kind acts. Not everyone cooperates with this process, but those who do can begin to look beyond themselves. Couples who embrace the process will produce goodness and kindness, which our world yearns for.

FAITHFULNESS

A person can be faithful in a lot of things. This fruit is not about faithfully making day trades, playing video games, or keeping up a Snapstreak on Snapchat. It is about faithfulness in relationships both with God and with others. In a sense, everyone practices faithfulness; it's what you are devoted to. Some people are devoted to things that simply do not matter. Those things may change as they lose their appeal over time, and new practices gain appeal. So ask yourself, *What is he faithful to? Or where can I find evidence of her devotion?*

---

3 Proverbs 15:1, NASB95
4 Ephesians 4:32, NASB95

This is why it's a good idea to date for a while before tying the knot. Nearly anyone can exhibit these traits for a weekend, but practicing them faithfully is another matter entirely. Look for evidence of the right habits over the long haul to ensure this person will be faithful not only to you – that's certainly important – but also to the things that truly matter.

GENTLENESS

No one wants to be around Oscar the Grouch all the time! Gentleness is a trait that leads to the right approach with people. If you are dating someone who is gruff and rude all the time, don't make excuses for that behavior! If he blows up at his mom, you don't say, "She deserved it for being nosy." If she is rude to a cashier, don't defend it! That lack of gentleness will either turn toward you, or you will always hear the conflict doled out to others. If that happens, it will be hard to keep friends, you'll end up alone, and harsh behavior will eventually be directed at you anyway. Scripture tells us to let our "gentle spirit be known to all men."[5] If it isn't evident, look for an exit.

SELF-CONTROL

Self-control snuck in at the end! Many may wish this one was not included but think about it. Do you really want to date someone without it? Self-control isn't really evident until it has been lost. It's about a breaking point. A twig can be snapped with little effort, but a lead pipe is tough to break. A person with a high breaking point will be more stable, and so will your relationship. But a lack of self-control leads to vulnerability. Consider this proverb: Like a city that is broken into and without walls is a man who has no control over his

---

5   Philippians 4:5, NASB95

spirit."[6] If you see someone without self-control, don't move into the city with him!

Note the first and last items on the Fruit of the Spirit list. They are like bookends that keep all these traits in line. Love is the motivation; self-control is the maintenance. Practicing these traits in any disciplined way requires self-control. Without it, personal growth in these areas will be stunted and irregular. It's like getting those weird-looking deformed fruits at the market for half price. They're called "seconds," and they look alien, weird, and sometimes diseased. Somehow the plant could not maintain consistent, healthy growth in the fruit. Self-control is that consistent set of instructions that keeps healthy growth consistent, steady, and sure.

YOUR WILL OR GOD'S?

The problem is that you may be using a different list than the Fruit of the Spirit listed above. You might not say so out loud, but you have another list that is more important. It takes priority over the Fruit of the Spirit. Guys, if a woman is a ten on the outside, but she doesn't display the Fruit of the Spirit, what do you do? If you're like most, you'll make excuses about her character as you give her your heart and passion. It'll eventually make you miserable, and it will slowly bleed the life force out of your own character. Ladies, what if a guy comes along and checks every box on the Fruit of the Spirit – this guy is a man of character – but he doesn't measure up physically or financially. Many women would say, "Oh, it's just not God's will for us to be together." You may be throwing away the man God has brought you! Don't get me wrong. At least *some* physical attraction should be there, but we put far too much emphasis on external features that don't last over

---
6   Proverbs 25:28, NASB95

a person's lasting character. And we wonder why so many people are miserable in their relationships!

MODEL WHAT YOU'RE LOOKING FOR

So, what happens when you find a person who does model the Fruit of the Spirit. If it's there, it didn't get there by accident. Any person who exhibits the Fruit of the Spirit has been diligently working on character and will be looking for it in YOU! Maybe God hasn't brought Mr. Right your way because He's waiting for you to be ready for him. Maybe that woman of character already came by, fellas, and she didn't see those traits modeled by you. This green flag states that you BOTH exhibit the Fruit of the Spirit. Ensure that it's evident in you even as you look for it in someone else.

> *"This green flag states that you BOTH exhibit the Fruit of the Spirit."*

CONCLUSION

If character is not what attracts you, something is wrong. Run. Flee. Heed the flag. Someone had gone before you and said, "I have seen great pain come from this circumstance." It's a warning!

Character is deeply formed, much like a diamond in the depths of the earth. Diamonds themselves are formed under intense pressure. It's no picnic creating a gem of incredible value. Maybe you've had some bad experiences dating people whose character has led to significant pain. Maybe your own character has caused much heartache. Do not despair! Those bad experiences are a form of pressure in your own life, and diamonds are being formed. They can be if you are willing to pay attention to the flags. Heed them now and pay attention to character. When the right gem comes along, you'll be ready.

CHAPTER TWO

EXPECTATION FLAGS

Who does the dishes? Toilet seat up or down? How long will your mother-in-law typically stay during visits? Every relationship carries with it a set of expectations that people hold, and the marriage relationship is no different. "Whoa, marriage?" you might say. Yes, you could call it one of my expectations. If you are watching the flags to find the right person, it isn't simply to date for a little while and then move on. At some point, you're playing for keeps, and when you do, you'll discover a host of expectations that you didn't even know you had. The only way to discover those expectations is when they aren't met. Marriage refines you partly by holding your expectations up and challenging you to figure out why they weren't met. It could be a problem with you or communication or unrealistic ideals. These struggles are normal, but marriage is worth the effort.

Some expectations, however, must be handled before you ever tie the knot. These are important expectation flags – two green and one red – that you want to get right because if you don't, you will be in for a heap of sorrow. Most of the big expectations are so obvious that they aren't being listed. For example, ladies, you expect that he won't cheat on you (see Fruit of the Spirit – faithfulness). And guys, you expect that she's cool with four hours of late-night Call of Duty online with your friends a few times a week (Kidding. Don't expect that!). The flags below are the less-obvious big ones representing traps that others have unwittingly fallen into or positive signs that many don't know enough to appreciate.

🚩 Green Flag: You can confidently show up as your authentic self

Do you know those excited butterflies that exist at the beginning of a relationship? They can influence us to do a lot. You start dressing differently, applying makeup with more care, digging out that bottle of cologne that she might like, putting up a public post that only he would get, and sending ridiculous emojis designed only for middle schoolers and those caught up in the early shoots of a budding romance. Yeah, people change a bit because they're giddy with a new relationship.

That's fine for a while, but eventually, you must be yourself. That doesn't mean you never improve[1], but that your own personality – your emotions, will, and style – should not be absorbed by your future spouse. A spouse brings out the best in you. The rough edges of your character become refined so that the unique features you possess stand prominently and

---

[1] See chapter seven on personal growth

display the work of art you are. You must be able to be who you are.

> "... become comfortable with who you are before you date someone."

Don't become someone else. It will wear you out. Does she have to dress you as though you are a representative of her? If she starts telling you how to dress now while you're just dating, she'll tell you for the rest of your life. Ladies, do you allow him to obsess with the outside rather than the inside? If he's that obsessed with the outside, then maybe it's just your outside that he's obsessed with. And if you respond by dressing with more emphasis on the outside, perhaps even adjusting the angle of your selfies just for him, you are only feeding into the problem. External beauty fades (just ask your Great Aunt Thelma), and so will his interest. Many people come into a relationship with such low self-esteem that they become willing participants who change themselves to fit the expectations of their significant other.

It is a self-esteem issue, and people conform themselves according to someone else's expectations, thinking they will like themselves better, too. They won't because this sort of accommodation is artificial and awkward. If you contort yourself like this, you'll either eventually go back to your original self, which your spouse won't like, or you'll stay uncomfortable, which leaves you in self-loathing and without respect from your spouse. If you are an extension of him or her, there's nothing unique about you to appreciate.

The best way to see this flag is to become comfortable with who you are *before* you date someone. Learn to love yourself without someone's sweet talk. Discover what God says about

> *"Marriage doesn't fix you; it only amplifies what you already have."*

you and develop the self-confidence to maintain your authentic self while in a serious relationship.

🚩 **Red Flag:** **When you expect marriage to fix the person**

Marriage is sometimes like a gigantic mirror that is held up to your face, revealing your flaws; it's similar to using the restroom while out somewhere and discovering hair askew, a rogue pimple, and the occasional lettuce leaf between your teeth. Don't get me wrong: marriage is great! But within that amazing relationship, we discover our own flaws and are refined over time. That happens naturally, so you can expect both you and your marriage partner to undergo some positive changes even if those changes are sometimes uncomfortable. What you cannot expect is that marriage will solve some gaping character flaw in your spouse just because you were willing to marry a person who consistently sent strong signals of insecurity and selfishness. If you do expect that, then the marriage mirror will one day shatter over your head!

Marriage doesn't fix you; it only amplifies what you already have. Many people hold to a fairy tale view of marriage in the fantasy that the flaws they see while dating can be papered over with a marriage license. These people become disillusioned over time, never having the intimate relationship they dreamed of but rather slowly drifting apart in an uneasy marriage or ending that marriage in divorce. Save yourself the pain and be honest about real flaws. If they are present in the dating phase, a ring isn't going to change much. If you see marriage as a solution to a character problem or a personality flaw, you are setting yourself up for disappointment.

Marriage is not like the plotline of a children's movie where even the bad guy was just a misunderstood person who turned good in the end. Well, maybe in 0.00001% of marriages, that can happen, but this book is for the 99.99999% of people, including you. Plan on the person you marry to be the exact same person throughout your marriage. Scratch that. Plan on the person you marry no longer having to impress you and deciding to no longer care about the bad habits and idiosyncrasies you thought would disappear magically during the honeymoon. A few negative qualities may improve over time, but you don't get to pick which ones those are, and the others will often trend worse.

Do you tell yourself he'll stop hanging out late with his boys most nights once you get married? Do you think she'll stop bossing you around after the ceremony? You won't even have to wait until the reception to awaken from that dream. The people you date tell you, through their actions, exactly who they are, and if you believe there will be a dramatic change brought on by marital bliss, you are sadly mistaken.

This is also a good time to consider your own character. What do your own actions say about who you are? If there is an area where you need to improve, it's time to stop making excuses – it's because of an ex or that psycho roommate or even parents – and start fixing the problem you have. Don't justify it; rectify it. Maybe it's a lying habit. You stretch the truth without even thinking. Or perhaps you're caught up in destructive behavior and have not been willing to include some outside help to finally do away with it. You might have a laziness issue that you have so far gotten away with, but which will cause real problems and frustrations in marriage. Whatever it is, don't let it go. If a problem is present when you're single, it will be amplified when you're married.

> **Green Flag: You both understand that marriage involves selflessness**

Because marriage amplifies what is already there, the mirror it holds up to you is a two-way mirror of a sort. Not only do you get the mirror, but that mirror is also a window into your spouse's soul. There is tremendous beauty in marriage, but there's also a whole lot of ugly. You'll find her at her worst; you'll see him at his lowest. Each of Snow White's dwarves will make appearances at inopportune times as you see your spouse act sleepy and dopey and grumpy and bashful – sometimes all at once! Then you'll discover the dwarves have cousins. Cranky, Foolish, and Leaves-His-Socks-Laying-Around-The-House will come to visit often. It is in those moments that your determination will be tested. Why did you get married in the first place? If it was for selfish reasons, you're in trouble and will need to learn on the job fast. In a healthy marriage, only a selfless attitude will do.

Marriage is an exercise in selflessness. You have committed yourself to the service industry, and you have one customer to please. The Bible describes this act of selflessness through instructions to the husbands:

> *Husbands, love your wives, just as Christ also loved the church and gave Himself up for her, so that He might sanctify her, having cleansed her by the washing of water with the word, that He might present to Himself*

the church in all her glory, having no spot or wrinkle or any such thing; but that she would be holy and blameless. So husbands ought also to love their own wives as their own bodies. He who loves his own wife loves himself.[2]

Selflessness involves giving up oneself for another, just as Jesus did. And how did He do that? By literally laying down His life! The goal is to make the other person better. These verses describe how the husband's sacrificial love is to make his wife better. Wives are directed a few verses earlier to do the same thing through a submissive spirit. Both are examples of selflessness.

If you cannot put someone else's needs ahead of your own, then don't get married! Stay single if you don't want to serve someone else because every day, you will need to practice putting your spouse ahead of yourself. There's no shame in singleness, and some people are even called to be single (God calls it a gift). But don't marry a girl and make her miserable because you don't want to serve her! Don't marry a guy if you can't get used to him getting on your nerves even as you accommodate him. This green flag comes with a cross attached, which you will carry every day.

Remember, though, that this is a green flag precisely because you BOTH come into marriage with this understanding of selflessness. Selflessness practiced alone without your spouse's own selflessness will be lonely and difficult to maintain, but when you have a partner in selflessness, beautiful things happen. You enjoy the benefit of someone caring for you in the same way that you express care. Your marriage will come

---

[2] Ephesians 5:25-28, NASB95

alive as you experience a depth of appreciation for the blessing that comes from this kind of selflessness. How can you make that happen? Ensure that you embrace selflessness and look for the same flag in your future spouse.

INTERLUDE

THE FIVE BUCKETS

There are five buckets that each person must have filled during childhood to function well in relationships. Each bucket relates to how we see ourselves, how we interact with others, and how we relate to change. Understanding what these buckets are is important before moving forward. Here are the five buckets:

THE VALUABLE BUCKET

If this bucket is filled, you will understand that you have value. If you have value, you have worth, and you will treat yourself accordingly because you have healthy self-esteem.

If this bucket is not filled, either you will view yourself as cheap or worthless, basing your value on external factors like performance, or you will have an inflated view of your own value that prevents you from seeing yourself properly.

We treat things based on their value. Cheap stuff is easily tossed, and we don't care if it gets damaged or destroyed. It's cheap, so who cares? What happens when a person sees herself as cheap? She allows herself to be treated differently, like one without value. She will derive her value based on how others consider her. This opens her up to exploitation and to lowering her own personal standards for the sake of feeling like she matters. She will often feel even less valuable. A man will respond in a similar way if he doesn't see himself as valuable. He will often engage in self-destructive behavior because nothing seems to matter. Who cares if binge drinking destroys him? What's the problem with his insane driving? He will only make his problem worse.

Seeing your value means you know that you matter. You are important, not because others say so but because God says so. This bucket initially gets filled through parents, but it ultimately can only be filled by God.[1] People who understand their value will treat themselves with respect, allowing them to center their lives on what matters. They will also be able to treat others with value. If you have trouble treating others with value – if you find yourself finding fault with others and writing others off – could it be that you need to start with understanding your own value? Then you'll be able to see the value in others.

THE VULNERABLE BUCKET

If this bucket is filled, you are able to share about yourself with an appropriate amount of vulnerability. You're okay with a few chinks in your armor, knowing that there is no way for people to get close to you without seeing them.

---

[1] See the Spiritual Flags in chapter six to learn three things that people try to get from others but can only get from God.

If this bucket is not filled, you will not be aware of what makes you vulnerable. Consequently, you will lack self-restraint or the understanding to prevent further damage, leading to resentment and rage issues.

Vulnerability admits that we are all works in progress, and we all rely on each other. Although some people exploit the vulnerabilities of others, most are simply trying to make their way through life with their own flaws. The mutual trust that flows from this allows people to inspect their own lives and see not only the natural imperfections but also dangerous areas of behavior that could lead to further harm. Then, to avoid the consequences that could come from unchecked flaws, those who know their vulnerabilities don't simply live with them; they slowly make improvements.

THE IMPERFECT BUCKET

If this bucket is filled, you are able to pursue goals and understand boundaries with the realization that failure will occur. When it does, you can notice and correct it or learn to live with it.

If this bucket is not filled, you are either a goodie-two-shoes or a rule breaker. You either value or abhor perfection.

Embracing imperfection means being okay with failure. It's a sign that you grew up in a home with reasonable boundaries, and when you crossed them, your parents gave appropriate discipline. The emphasis was on trying, even if many attempts were unsuccessful. Whether in pursuing dreams or simply following the rules, the right amount of personal independence and supportive structure allows children to become adults who can handle failure. Many have not had this kind of environ-

> *"Enjoying deeper relationships often means asking for help."*

ment. The rules may be ultra-rigid or never defined, rarely enforced, or wildly unpredictable. The result is that some people will struggle either with having an independent spirit or creating the structural framework. They are either too timid to branch out or too disgusted to follow the rules. If the imperfect bucket is full, you will likely accomplish much more in life.

THE DEPENDENT BUCKET

If this bucket is filled, you are able to live comfortably within a community framework and have a healthy reliance on others to have your needs met.

If this bucket is not filled, you are either characterized by neediness, which drains others, or you cannot accept help and never make your needs known.

Dependence involves interdependence, the realization that within relationships, needs are constantly expressed and met among people. This is a hallmark of humanity. When children see their needs met and grow in their own responsibility over time, they are well adapted to the right level of dependence. If children somehow see themselves as a burden to their parents or if they are continually overindulged, they may respond by drastically increasing or decreasing their dependence level. It is impossible to be in a relationship with someone who continually needs something from you. It may feel nice for a bit, but it sucks the energy out of you. Others go to the opposite extreme and are an emotional wall. Ask them if they need help, and they'll let you know they've "got it." Their emotional independence makes it difficult to connect with others. Enjoying deeper relationships often means asking for help.

THE SPONTANEOUS & OPEN BUCKET

If this bucket is filled, you can thrive in a stable setting but also handle spontaneous changes.

If this bucket is not filled, you will gravitate to extremes and become either hyper-controlling over others or a free-wheeling spirit who lacks control.

Life isn't living without some measure of spontaneity. The rules matter. Having a sense of order and stability is important, but those spontaneous exceptions to the rules bring vitality. If you have been given the right level of control as a child, you can live within a good balance of stability and spontaneity. Without that right level – a situation where there is either more or less control – you will likely gravitate toward being controlling or being a free spirit who refuses to be pinned down. These extremes become a problem for relationships because life is meant for flexibility within structure.

Some people just cannot handle that. Rules are rules, and they derive meaning from a strictly-ordered life. People around them suffer, but they will accept nothing less than rigid structure. When problems come, it is easy for them to blame their spouse, who was not disciplined enough.

Others are so spontaneous that they are off the charts. You never know what new thing they will take up, and you can never count on them to adhere to a schedule. They are ready to pick up and move to Timbuktu at the drop of a hat. When problems arise in a marriage, they believe their spouse is too

> *"Adding to someone else's bucket does not take away from our own."*

controlling, but it is they who are unable to hold any commitments.

The appropriate level of control is not found in the extremes. If you came from those fringes, this might be difficult for you. When you parent your own children, give them the right level of control, making expectations clear while allowing room for failure. Guide your children without controlling their personalities so they can learn the right level of spontaneity.

EMPTY BUCKETS?

With healthy parenting, each of these five buckets will be filled by age twelve. Otherwise, you will seek relationships and other sources to fill what is lacking. Most people do this without even realizing they are. You may have noticed that we live in a fallen world full of problems, and that means most of us have buckets that have not been filled all the way.

If your buckets aren't full, this will affect your relationships and your parenting. There's a generational impact that comes from empty or half-filled buckets. Your buckets are filled so that you can fill those of others. Each of our interactions can help fill someone's bucket or take away from it. Adding to someone else's bucket does not take away from our own. Instead, we simply point them to what filled our bucket, like bringing someone to the tree where you got your basketful of apples and picking a couple choice fruits for them. This is most true for children, who cannot fill the buckets themselves. If the parents have filled buckets, they can pour into their children to give them what they need. Otherwise, the children are neglected while the parents continue unhelpful ways to fill the empty buckets of their own childhoods.

The next chapter will cover what to do and what not to do if your buckets weren't filled. This is not a mortal wound, but untreated, it will lead to you wounding others and feeling wounded without knowing why. So read on, O brave one, and fill your buckets!

CHAPTER THREE

RELATIONAL FLAGS

Broken people interact in broken ways. Healthy people interact in healthy ways. One leads to a painful spiral downward, while the other creates an uplifting environment of support and even fun. The flags in this chapter will set the tone of your relationship and the positive or negative environment that you'll see daily. You want to be able to connect deeply with someone without fighting the noise of unspoken hurts or misplaced wants. From the outset, you should know that we are all broken in some way or another, but don't despair! Our God – the God of grace and mercy – provides healing and hope, allowing us to move toward relational health. Read on to discover the promises and perils of the relational flags so that you, too, can be in great relational shape and spot relational health in your significant other.

> **Green Flag: You're both aware of the five buckets, and you're on your way to getting them refilled**

You just read about the five buckets in the interlude before this chapter. Neglected buckets in our childhood will plague our relationships in adulthood. Because this world is fallen, people come into relationships with brokenness that they aren't even aware of. Do you know that one guy who walks into a room full of people and has no concept of volume control and begins talking to one person so loudly that everyone is annoyed?[1] Broken people in a relationship are like that. Everyone else knows there is an issue, but the broken person doesn't realize it. Life's relationships are seen as a place where the buckets can be refilled.

But they can't. The relationships will only multiply the evidence of empty buckets in your life and will multiply the brokenness you're experiencing. This will impact future generations, too, because children will be most impacted by parents with empty buckets.

This is why you must take responsibility for your buckets. Now. So they weren't filled when you were eight years old. What's your plan? Are you going to sue your parents for it? Even if you won a legal judgment, your buckets would still be empty. The only thing you can do is own the problem and fill your buckets the right way.

So don't make excuses. Don't justify your own behavior because you claim you didn't get what you need. That's how the cycle continues, leading to broken relationships and empty buckets.

The first step toward getting your buckets refilled is to take responsibility for the issues you face. Since you are no longer a seven-year-old, you must own them and recognize

---

[1] If you don't know what I mean, maybe YOU are that guy!

the fact that, although those deficiencies were not caused by you, the relational problems you have experienced were your doing. "But he was the womanizer," you reply. Then how did you end up with him? Or you declare, "But she never would let me be me." Don't you realize that issue started at the beginning of the relationship, and you liked it because you thought it was filling your bucket? The point is that even the relational problems caused by the *other* person still reflect something about you. If your exes were so crazy, your willingness to enter into relationships with them is telling.

> *"The point is that even the relational problems caused by the other person still reflect something about you."*

Once you have taken responsibility for your empty buckets, you can begin to fill them, but beware where you go to fill them! If your dependence bucket was never filled, then you struggle either with never asking for help for anything or with always asking for help in everything. Whichever one you are, God will likely lead you to your opposite. So, guys, you may try to do everything on your own because you consider it a weakness to ask for help, and you are likely to date a lady who will ask you for help with every little thing. You'll be annoyed and wonder why she can't solve her own problems, and she'll wear you down. Not only do you have too much to handle on your own (because you don't know how to ask for help), but also you'll have to take her needs on to yourself. Ladies, if you're the independent type, a needy guy will likely turn you off unless you artificially fill your bucket by taking on his needs. The people you date or marry are not equipped to fill your buckets on their own. They do play a role to help, but it's a big bucket, and they can't be expected to fill it up alone.

God is our bucket Filler. The truth in His Word is the best way to get our buckets refilled. Spending time with others who follow Jesus and studying the Bible together will correct those wrong perspectives you have, repairing your bucket as you fill it. Filling a bucket is not unlike eating when you're hungry. Sure, you *could* fill up on potato chips or other junk food, but that full feeling won't last long, and you'll likely feel much worse. That's why truth is important in this process because only the truth of God will last in your bucket.

When you both understand the buckets and are working on getting them filled, two things will occur. First, your relationship will improve as you maintain a healthy outlook on how to fill your buckets, allowing you to see positive results. Second, when issues arise, you'll begin to look at the problem with a bucket mindset. Maybe she seems uptight about company coming over because she doesn't feel valuable and finds her value in how the house looks for others. So you clean the counter and give her some praise instead of becoming upset with her. Maybe his empty "imperfect" bucket is why he can't seem to get excited about a new job opportunity. He thinks he must knock it out of the park, so he can't even update his resume. You can give him a little nudge and remind him that perfection isn't required.

🚩 Red Flag: They love bomb you

Beware the love bomb! The love bomb is a dirty bomb disguised as a trojan horse. It looks good, seems innocent, and is genuinely fun, but it's toxic. The love bomb occurs when your new boyfriend or girlfriend floods you with attention, gifts, special experiences, and signs of affection – all very early in a relationship. It's like drinking from a fire hydrant. There's a seemingly endless supply of affection – much more than you can take in – yet it's more than a little dangerous.

Love bombers bomb for a reason. They are hiding their own character flaws. Who has time to get to know someone when there are so many surface-level displays of affection to enjoy? It's hard to get to know a love bomber; this is intentional, even if the love bomber is unaware of it. All that affection serves as a giant mask to keep you from getting to know them and spotting red flags. Rushing into sexual activity can be one form of love bombing. What is meant to be slow and released at the right time, after marriage, is instead set on full blast right up front.

Who falls for the love bomb? Desperate people do. People are surprised and flattered by all that attention – someone is literally obsessed with them – and in desperation, they receive it without question and assume they've hit the jackpot. Finally, someone is into me, and it's love at first sight! Face the facts: nobody is going to be that into you, nor should they be. Let them make a big deal out of a milestone birthday, but unless you're a member of the royal family, you should be suspicious of someone treating you like a queen every single day.

Desperate people will even post all the love bombing they receive on social media, believing the attention is good. They are unwittingly sharing that they are being bombarded.

"He brought me flowers."

"He took off work to surprise me for lunch. Then he took me to a fancy restaurant, and afterward, we went to a club."

> *"... the love bomb can be seen for what it is: a desperate smoke screen designed to hide one's own insecurities while taking advantage of another's."*

"He bought me a Shih Tzu and took me out for sushi after treating me to a shiatsu massage."

And how long have you been dating? Four days? You're getting love bombed. He will sweep you off your feet because you are desperate, and you have no idea who he is. At least you know that, unless he bought gobs of Bitcoin in 2014, he just blew out his savings to impress you; he may be just as desperate as you are and needs to fill some of his buckets.

How do you avoid getting love bombed? First, handle your own insecurities properly so that you aren't desperate and vulnerable to the attack. Get to the point where you are confident in who you are. Then set a standard of pacing in a relationship without giving in to excessive attention. Finally, make it a habit to get to know who a person is with the appropriate level of self-disclosure for a new relationship. Then the love bomb can be seen for what it is: a desperate smoke screen designed to hide one's own insecurities while taking advantage of another's.

▶ **Green Flag: You talk for hours without knowing the time has passed**

"I love you more."

"No, I love *you* more."

Ugh. Okay, this deserves some explanation. This green flag matters because some people are just not compatible. I don't even like putting it that way because it suggests a weird, cosmic compatibility formula that doesn't exist. What I mean is that some people never really connect with a boyfriend or girlfriend but still get married. This is not good. It's a desperation play from those convinced they will never connect with someone, leading them to settle for something less than a deep relationship. Some sort of connection must exist for the relationship to be fulfilling.

But it goes deeper than that. The relationship must connect on some sort of deep level. Something must be there for a marriage to attach itself to. Common goals, dreams, mutual faith, or core values had better be there, or else you've got a superficial marriage waiting to happen.

Superficial marriages lead to separate dreams, separate lifestyles, and separate bedrooms. No one will stop you from tying the knot, but that knot will be like a five-year-old's first attempt at tying his shoe if your relationship doesn't connect to something deep. It will quickly come loose. The ability to talk for hours is a sign that you have a relationship that is not superficial, that you can talk about matters of substance, goals, aspirations, and plans.

HOW TO TALK FOR HOURS

Consider these tips for developing a relationship that connects on a deep level:

Genuine interest. You both indicate interest in each other's background, pursuits, and goals. This involves paying attention to the little things, asking questions, and remembering conversations. Why is it difficult to talk to a person in the elevator? Because you have no shared understanding of each other. That understanding comes when you get to know someone; doing so with genuine interest is crucial to getting conversations more exciting than the ones on an elevator.

Willingness to share. A relationship must grow two ways rather than one. In other words, you both must be willing to share your lives with each other. If you do not tell your story, you will short circuit the relationship. Sharing about yourself includes expressing the painful bits, too. This should, of course, be done in an appropriate way. Don't pour out all of your childhood trauma on the first date, but do share even the difficult parts of your past as appropriate.

Honesty. Some people have the habit of stretching the truth or even manufacturing it out of thin air! Connecting deeply means doing so in an honest way. If you struggle with telling the truth, you'll find yourself in trouble rather quickly. If you embellish stories just to impress a girl, she will be far less impressed when she finds out they are not true. Save yourself the trouble and the heartache.

Lack of distractions. It's great that you have a cool phone and all, but phones aren't fun to date. Make a habit of removing the phone and other distractions so that you can focus on getting to know your boyfriend or girlfriend. This concept could have its own chapter or at least a flag. Just know that our world has been progressively becoming more distracted, and those distractions prevent us from thinking deeply and connecting deeply with others. Don't let distractions stifle a great relationship.

Mix up the depth. If you only talk about surface-level things, you will both eventually get bored (and find some distractions to keep your sanity). Discussing only deep matters does not work well because those topics ought to connect with real things, which are on the surface. So mix it up. This is where *why* questions come in handy. Occasionally notice something and ask, "Why?" You may be surprised by the answer you receive and where it takes the conversation.

IT'S WORTH IT

You may feel overwhelmed by buckets, bombs, and a boatload of conversation, but remember, you are seeking the most intimate and fulfilling human relationship that you will have. This is not the sort of thing you want to get wrong. The rewards are available to the couple who will choose wisely, stay relationally healthy, and connect deeply. Keep that worthy end in mind.

CHAPTER FOUR

EMOTIONAL FLAGS

Our emotions affect everything else. They impact our will, our dreams, our mood, and on and on. Some people don't realize the importance of nurturing their own emotions in a healthy way and walk directly into a trap that saps them of their emotional reservoir and stunts their own development. If you cannot be emotionally free with someone so important to your life, you'll wind up in a prison. Freedom will seem so close beyond the bars in front of you, but you cannot get there. Emotional flags represent the biggest positive and negative potential for emotional well-being in a relationship.

> **Red Flag: You don't feel safe, and you change who you are to fit them**

When a person decides to date you, shouldn't it be you they date? This natural expectation does not always play out. Some

> "Never let someone change who you are to match something other than what God has called you to be."

people have an idea of the person they want to date, and you aren't it. Nevertheless, you've found yourself in a relationship with someone who has placed your face on a mythical conception of a person. Most people, when in a healthy relationship, will realize they are dating a normal person and adjust their expectations (we all have unrealistic ones) to match who the other person is. The red flag exists when someone is so entrenched in a preconceived idea of who you should be that you change who you are to match it. This is why it is so important for you to be confident in who you are before you ever get into a dating relationship. If you do not, you may carve away your own personality only to realize years later that you are an empty husk.

God created you with a specific design in mind. Your personality, upbringing, and temperament have combined in a way that makes you who you are. When someone else comes in with another idea of your identity, it creates a conflict between God's identity for you and that of someone else. Never let someone change who you are to match something other than what God has called you to be.

This does not mean you do not have areas where you can improve. A boyfriend, girlfriend, or spouse can and will naturally reveal areas of improvement. That will happen without you trying a thing. We live in a fallen world, and there are many things about our character that do not align with God's best for us. So how can you differentiate changes in behavior that bring real improvement from those that are conformity to something unnatural?

When someone wants you to change, it should be to make you closer to the person God created you to be. The red flag exists here because many people manipulate a person to conform not to God's design but to their own flawed expectations for you.

If you conform to another person's will, you will be guilty of two things. First, you will reject God's design for you to match someone else's design, essentially placing the other person before God. That's not good and will only lead to problems. Second, you will warp your own understanding to fit someone else's understanding, which robs you of the ability to make decisions and depletes your will.

The advice here is to let God be God. If someone has another design for you, demand that it be described in biblical terms. If not, you'll conform to someone else's whims, but it won't be just you. Most marriages produce children, so unless you can set the right boundaries, your children, current or future, will be controlled by someone with a domineering ideal for people in their orbit. This flag is not a single but a double one because it will not simply impact you but will have repercussions on your offspring. God has an ideal for each person, and you do not want that ideal to be hijacked by anyone else. If you are with someone who demands changes to fit some preconceived notion, it's a major red flag.

Let's also address the other part of this red flag: you don't feel safe. There may be a fear of physical safety, which is an obvious warning to get out of such a relationship! Other fears persist, however, which are also major concerns. There will not be a conversation in which your sweetie says, "I would like you to change who you are to suit me." It's always more subtle than that, but there are some not-so-subtle behaviors to watch for. If he asserts his will over yours in every situation – goes over you every time – you find yourself simply doing whatever he says to avoid conflict. You go along to get along in just about every situation. Compromise is important in a relationship, but this is one-sided. A guy who conforms his decision to whatever his girlfriend wants just to avoid an argument may think he's keeping the peace, but he's slowly giving a piece of himself away each time, losing his own uniqueness and individuality.

Do you think that will be cool in ten years? If out of fear or comfort, you decide to essentially give up your will to another person, you'll despise yourself one day. Giving in to emotional manipulation is not a recipe for relational bliss. Both parties in a relationship should give of themselves and consider the needs of the other. To avoid this flag, practice healthy compromise early and often. You will sometimes be more accommodating to him, and sometimes he will be to you. That's normal, too. If there's no compromise, there's no future.

> **Red Flag: They start dating you without getting over their ex**

God is the Author of time. He created it – and the world – and you. Yet somehow, we get in a rush and think that time is something we must control and handle. That notion leads us to rush into things without thinking through all the important factors that are involved. It's how mistakes are not simply made but compounded. That multiplies trouble.

People who begin to date before getting over an ex are bound to multiply trouble. There are life lessons to be learned in plain sight, but the emotional pain of a recent breakup is too strong. Instead, mistakes are repeated on a faster and stronger scale, and you are just along for the ride.

People who get into this situation are often desperate. Although this warning flag is waving prominently, they believe that they can somehow stave off the disaster that is to come through their own availability or listening ear. This red flag exists not because of an availability issue but because of a maturity issue. If a guy isn't over a bad breakup, he needs time to consider what happened so that he can grow and mature as a result. If not, he'll either repeat the same mistakes or overcompensate by making all new ones.

Do you remember the freezing weather and snowstorm that hit Texas in 2021? Dallas Fort Worth Airport measured five inches of snow – in Dallas! – and it was pandemonium. If you're riding with a driver in the snow, would you want that driver to have grown up in Texas or in Wisconsin? Most native Texans have little experience driving in snow, but up north, they'll get five inches and not even bother canceling school. If you are driving in the snow and lose traction, your car will spin out unless you make a correction. Speeding up or hitting the brakes won't solve the problem; steering is the issue. Turn the wheel one way, and you'll make the problem worse. Turn it the other way, and you'll get back on track. This takes experience though, because small corrections are the key. If a driver overcorrects, the problem will reverse itself, which is why a driver who is inexperienced with snow may

> *"If a person needs you to bring stability, disaster is coming."*

careen wildly right and left before finally connecting with a light pole.

A person who has just been in a breakup is like a Texan driving in a snowstorm. He has a traction issue in life. Will he spin out? Overcorrect? Hopefully not, but don't ride shotgun with him! Wait until he regains control by truly getting over his ex and learning whatever lessons should be learned. This is not the kind of thrill ride you want. Relationships only work well when they are stable.

People who ignore this red flag do so because they are used to the turmoil. They think it's normal for a life to veer left and right, out of control and hitting poles. In their own inexperience and desperation, they believe they will be the voice of reason that keeps a person stable. Don't do it. You can't fix her. If a person needs *you* to bring stability, disaster is coming. Look at your own life and what's falling apart. You are with yourself 24/7, and you're struggling. How are you going to fix someone else? People need their own stability before they are ready to date someone, or else there will be turmoil.

The healing that's needed can only come from God. If you get yourself into His Word and talk with God, and if you spend time with others doing the same thing – such as at church and in Bible study – you'll be able to make those little corrections that give your life traction again. Instead of rushing into another relationship, run to God. Learn to love Him so that you can love yourself. Only then can you learn to love someone else who is at the same point.

Love is patient.[1] It's willing to wait. Not being willing to wait is a sign of desperation. It says that you cannot wait to heal from pain or even trust God's timing. If you blow past the red flags and date someone who also needs healing, you are, in essence taking control and telling God, "I can't wait on Your timing." It ultimately displays a lack of trust in God. Take a step back and be patient. Let God work, and you'll be amazed at what He does and by whom He brings your way.

▶ Green Flag: You care about what you can give more than about what you can get

"It is more blessed to give than to receive."[2] Tell that to an eight-year-old on Christmas. Kids only slowly get the concept, giving some glimpses of hope as they develop that they find joy in giving. Selflessness is a learned behavior, and many kids don't yet have it. That's normal, but by adulthood, the spirit of giving is meant to take over. It doesn't always happen, though, does it? We see some adults who have only ever learned to take, and we wonder what happened.

You don't want to date a taker. That person entered into a relationship with you thinking only of what he could get. Maybe it was status because he wanted a little arm candy to impress others and increase his own standing. Or he was lonely or wanted physical intimacy or didn't like to cook. Guys, maybe you are the arm candy for the girl! If you start off buying her jewelry, she might cozy up to you and make you feel good and manly just so you'll open up your wallet for some more bling. Or she might just need someone to control. You'll do nicely. Avoid the trap, and don't date a taker.

---

[1] 1 Corinthians 13 is called the love chapter. Look it up to see all the amazing descriptions of love.
[2] This quote comes from the Bible; look up Acts 20:35.

A relationship can be balanced or imbalanced on this front. Sometimes two takers end up dating. It's not a pretty sight because they are both always clawing at each other for what the other won't give. Have you ever seen a miserable couple and said, "Those two deserve each other"? Yep, they're both takers who will be perpetually disgruntled until their relationship blows up. That's not the worst scenario.

What's worse is when there is an imbalance. If you come into a relationship ready to give, but you find yourself dating someone who only wants to take, you're in for a steady stream of manipulation. You'll find it difficult not to keep on giving, and you'll feel guilty whenever you consider a breakup. So you stay in the relationship because of a false sense of guilt, and you'll feel like a martyr while you slowly give up your soul to someone.

People develop all kinds of ulterior motives for dating a person. Maybe dating her increases your status or gives the impression that you have it all together. Or because your friends are no longer single, dating him allows you to stay in your friend group. Besides, he's athletic, and the kids will be adorable! If the relationship is more about what you can get than what you can give, at best, it will become a bland, stale marriage of convenience. You'll feel more like business partners than marriage partners. If you start a family, your kids will grow up with a warped understanding of what a loving relationship is meant to be.

Both parties must come into a relationship with the intention of giving rather than getting. Jesus' model of love for the Church – His bride, the Bible says – is to give Himself up to make her better. The relationship that becomes an opportunity to serve the other and make someone better follows the standard that Jesus set. Marriage is an opportunity to serve, to fold his laundry, to wash her dishes, to pick up the slack when he's meeting a work deadline, to accommodate a concern that she has even though you don't get it. Ironically, the happiest marriages always involve mutual service toward each other.

If your shared goal is giving, you both will receive. You will get a lot, and you will find tremendous satisfaction not only in the getting but also in the giving. You will find joy in otherwise mundane tasks for the simple satisfaction of knowing you are bettering your spouse. You will learn to enjoy all that life gives and align your heart more with God's design for getting the most out of life.

If your goal is getting, you will get little, and your relationship will be an emotional desert of scarcity. Instead of joyfully giving with little expectation of getting, you will become miserly with what you give and demanding of what you expect to get. Embittered, you will find your heart far from God's design to maximize joy in life. Indeed, there will be no joy found in what little you get because you will find yourself deserving of that and more.

PRACTICE THANKFULNESS

Thankfulness is a surprising safeguard against emotional pitfalls. When you find yourself single, even after a difficult breakup, thankfulness allows you to accept the opportunity to grow while out of the dating scene for a time. It becomes a healing balm on your soul because it expresses confidence that God is orchestrating your circumstances for good. Thankfulness will help you develop a positive self-image that will guard you against changing the core part of your identity just because someone has another idea of how you should look in a relationship. Thankfulness also adjusts your frame of mind to appreciate what you have and take away the desire to get rather than to give. It motivates our own expressions of giving and puts a layer of protection over an attitude that might otherwise sour. If you can be thankful and find someone who has also developed an attitude of thankfulness, your relationship can navigate away from the red emotional flags and toward the green.

CHAPTER FIVE

SEXUAL FLAGS

Okay, now we're getting to a more controversial part of this book. You may even be tempted to skip this chapter. You may also decide that you've gotten enough out of the book so far, and the sexual flags are negotiable. Maybe they aren't for everybody. These flags may work for some, you reason, but there are other options out there, other flags that can be followed for success in relationships without the sexual ethics of a bygone time. For that reason, please consider these reminders:

- ▶ The flags exist to help your relationship and not harm it. Green and red, they are there for your good.

- ▶ Each of the flags is restrictive. Red flags keep you from going somewhere you shouldn't, and green ones tell you the way you should go. Just like rules of the road keep cars moving without accidents, and restrictive train tracks keep the train in motion toward its destination, the flags all work to bring you to a good relational place by avoiding the danger zones.

▶ Some flags feel more restrictive than others. If you are near a particular marked danger zone, that's the zone where you may be tempted to downplay the danger. Some people have spent time in the red zone of the sexual flags, so it is harder to acknowledge the danger.

▶ The flags all come from truth and experience. The truth is found in God's Word, and the Bible is the best source to learn the truth about relationships and how they best function. The experience is from those who have gone before, who have seen the signs of bad relationships and say, "This red flag will help you avoid some of the relational pain the Bible warns against," or, "This green flag will help you attain some of the relational good the Bible offers."

Now let's get to these flags. You'll see there's really only one flag, and it's green.

▶ **Green Flag: You both realize purity leads to clarity and strive to remain pure**

Purity leads to clarity. That's the principle, and we want to pursue clarity. So what are purity and clarity?

Clarity is a condition that enables a person to see the truth about the world emotionally, intellectually, and spiritually. A person with clarity can understand life – can see better – than someone without clarity. Decision-making becomes easier, allowing the pursuit of the right goals. Clarity liberates the pocketbook for purchases that matter and leaves impulse buying in the dust. Clarity better aligns a person with the life God has designed.

Purity is the condition of sexual wholeness, free from degradation. A person who is sexually pure holds sexuality in very high regard and reserves sexual expression for marriage between a husband and wife. A description of what purity entails is included later in this chapter.

But wait! What if I'm not sexually pure now? What if I have given in to temptation in this area? Don't beat yourself up. Just like the other flags, a mistake in the past doesn't mean you cannot change things now. If you find yourself swimming in an area with a strong undertow, once you are alerted to the danger, you can leave, right? Regardless of your past, you can begin again. Fresh starts are allowed.

The opposite of purity is impurity, and the opposite of clarity is opacity, a fuzzy-thinking mind with a blurred conception of reality. Purity helps a person think clearly. It's not that purity is the magic bullet for clarity, but rather that impurity diminishes clarity and leads to a warped view of the world. The Bible backs this up. It says, "Flee immorality. Every other sin that a man commits is outside the body, but **the immoral man sins against his own body**."[1]

While all sin is destructive, sexual sin is more personal and with more immediate effects on a person. It affects one's psyche, which reduces clarity.

---

[1] 1 Corinthians 6:18, NASB95, emphasis added

The windshield of a car is at its best when it's clear. Have you ever taken a long road trip somewhere? Then you know what bugs will do to a windshield! One thing that is sure to obstruct your vision on the road is a windshield filled with the innards of recently-departed insects. Your windshield wipers don't clear away bugs so much as they smear them and make matters worse. The real solution is to get out and scrub off the bugs with a gas station squeegee.[2]

Sexual impurity is like a series of bugs getting smashed into a windshield. They might not seem so bad at first, but they progressively obscure any clarity you may have been seeking. Many people attempt to keep going and occasionally wipe the gunk away, but that often leads to blurrier vision. The real solution is to stop and refocus with a clean start.

That clean start begins with truths found in the Bible. Here are a few places where the Bible mentions this all-important topic.

- ▶ For the grace of God has appeared, bringing salvation to all men, instructing us to deny ungodliness and worldly desires and to live sensibly, righteously, and godly in the present age.[3]

- ▶ For this is the will of God, your sanctification; that is, that you abstain from sexual immorality; that each of you knows how to possess his own vessel in sanctification and honor, not in lustful passion, like the Gentiles who do not know God; and that no man

---

[2] By the way, clarity is not automatically granted because of sexual purity. Just like a windshield's view can be obstructed by many things – like pollen, rain, or even your own poor vision – a person's clarity must be maintained in multiple ways and even pursued in others. Sexual purity will prevent the loss of clarity, but a person should still continue to pursue additional habits that will increase clarity.

[3] Titus 2:11-12, NASB95

transgress and defraud his brother in the matter because the Lord is the avenger in all these things, just as we also told you before and solemnly warned you. For God has not called us for the purpose of impurity but in sanctification. So, he who rejects this is not rejecting man but the God who gives His Holy Spirit to you.[4]

> *"... by God's grace, a person can say no to temptations, including sexual ones."*

▶ But immorality or any impurity or greed must not even be named among you, as is proper among saints.[5]

Here is what we can learn from these passages. First, by God's grace, a person can say no to temptations, including sexual ones. By our own strength, most of us would be doomed to failure in this arena. We're swimming against the cultural current here. Although we find so many examples of people swimming in red-flagged waters, we also see the pain and heartache that comes from it; yet we are reminded that it is possible to avoid those areas and be happy. It IS possible!

It is also God's will. When we find something bigger to live for – God's plan for us – we put ourselves on a mission to avoid those sexual red flag areas. Notice the need for us to "learn to control" ourselves in these areas. If you thought it would come naturally, guess again! It will take time and patience and endurance and help, but everything worth doing takes time to learn. A baby learning to walk is developing skilled self-control. The same sorts of skills are learned by the

---

[4] 1Thessalonians 4:3-8, NASB95
[5] Ephesians 5:3, NASB95

nervous teenager behind the wheel of a car for the first time. Important things in life are worthwhile enough to work for. Your freedom from sexual snares is worth it, too, and it leads to clarity as you align yourself with God's will.

Think about that. Being aligned with God's will. Whew! That brings a rush. Find your groove and walk with confidence in God's plan for you.

This mission requires vigilance, too, because little things turn into big things. Little weeds in a garden soon grow and choke out a good plant, stunting its growth and stifling its production. We are told there must not even be a hint of sexual immorality, making it important to stop the little things before they even start. Since purity involves being free of any impurities, what should we look out for to stay by the green flags and avoid the red? The next flag will help you know what to look out for.

Red Flag: When you do anything else

This red flag is a bonus to help clarify the green flag. If purity leads to clarity, impurity leads to cloudiness – cloudy thinking, cloudy heart, cloudy mindset. Take note of the following practices that will steal away your purity:

PORNOGRAPHY

Both purity and clarity can be robbed quickly through viewing pornography. Porn is a thief because of the false picture it paints of sexual activity. Multiple attacks happen while viewing it. First, you train your brain for unnatural arousal as you seek kinkier stuff. Second, more natural arousal no longer happens because you have desensitized yourself to it. Neural research has shown the effect of being similar to that of drug addicts who seek harder drugs to chase the high they can no longer achieve with tamer stuff. Third, your expectations for real sexual activity become skewed, and you expect the unnatural from your partner, expecting her to behave like a paid performer.

It should also be noted that, although people try to say pornography is victimless, only affecting the viewer, this is not at all the case. It affects a future spouse who is married to a porn addict for one, which is a plenty-big deal. It also supports the porn industry, which is known for subjecting women to awful conditions by coercing them into performing and then creating a dependency to continue. Some are involved in human trafficking and slavery. That creates plenty of victims to go around.

You may not consume outright pornography, but there are other ways that images can rob us of our purity. One of the biggest can be found in streaming shows, movies, and social media, which have capitalized on the fact that sex sells. Sex scenes, nudity, and very skimpy clothing in these shows mean that to stay pure, a person must stay away.

Take a stand on this. Job gives a great example of this in the Bible. He said, "I have made a covenant with my eyes; how could I gaze at a virgin?"[6] Be strong, tell someone about this struggle, and begin taking real steps to overcome this area if it is a struggle for you. You are not alone in this. Countless people have felt overwhelmed by this vice but have found ways to overcome it.

---

6   Job 31:1, NASB95

WEAK OR UNDEFINED BOUNDARIES

You probably figured that staying sexually pure means not having sexual intercourse with someone, but that does lead to a question: What is allowed? There's a lot of potential activity between holding hands and outright sex. Somewhere there must be a line, right? Yes, there is, but people draw that line in different places.

The most important thing is to draw the line. Many don't. They explore a relationship with someone while only keeping a vague sense of boundaries, which they never discuss with the other person. If it does come up, they speak in euphemisms which makes boundaries fuzzy. Fuzzy doesn't lead to purity; fuzzy can't help with clarity. Draw a line. Consider the best place to draw a physical boundary that will keep you sexually pure. When you date, explain this to your boyfriend or girlfriend to state clearly where you draw the line. She might draw it sooner than you. If so, that's the new line for that relationship.

Beyond that, here are a few practical considerations:

Don't creep up to that line on your first date. If you come right up to the line on the first date, what's next? You're toast because you already got your motor revved up. Let the line be like a fence in the distance. You might come up to it on rare occasions, but be happy where you are.

Being sexually pure is about more than simply staying away from intercourse. Don't draw a line where you can somehow bring sexual pleasure to someone. That's not purity, which means you'll both lose clarity, which means you'll soon blow way past that line. Draw that line before arousal can happen.

Avoid being alone together. It's a lot harder to keep from crossing a line when you are alone. Make plans to be with friends or around others to avoid being overcome with temptation. Arrange your together time in public settings that allow you to talk alone but not be compromised.

CRUDE SPEECH AND LUSTFUL THOUGHTS

The way we speak and think has a way of compromising our purity mentally and emotionally, which means we'll have no chance physically. Do you think you can joke about sexual things and think about stuff that will get you aroused without affecting your purity? Don't weaken yourself like this. While speaking about sexual purity, the Bible says, "and there must be no filthiness and silly talk, or coarse jesting, which are not fitting, but rather giving of thanks."[7] If your speech is sexual, your mind will bend toward the sexual, and then your body will follow. Stop it early with your speech. By the way, this verse says that giving thanks is the antidote. Give it a try.

FORGETTING YOUR HERITAGE

You have a lot going for you, and many have gone before you. They are your heritage. You have a physical heritage in your family, and if you are a Christian, you have a spiritual heritage with Christians who have gone before you. The Bible describes these people in the book of Hebrews as a "cloud of witnesses," a group of people who are all cheering you on and standing as examples that temptation can be overcome. Faith can win. "Therefore, since we have so great a cloud of witnesses surrounding us, let us also lay aside every encumbrance and the sin which so easily entangles us, and let us run with endurance the race that is set before us, fixing our eyes on Jesus, the author, and perfecter of faith."[8] If it hinders

---
7   Ephesians 5:4, NASB95
8   Hebrews 12:1-2a, NASB95

you from running the race God has for you, get rid of it, along with anything sinful.

ISOLATION

Related to that verse above, becoming isolated makes us likely targets for weakening our willpower against impurity. Don't become isolated. The devil is described as a lion who roams around looking for his next victim to eat.[9] Which animal does a lion eat? The one that gets separated from the herd. Stay with your herd. Here's some great advice from God's Word on that: "Now flee from youthful lusts and pursue righteousness, faith, love, and peace, with those who call on the Lord from a pure heart."[10] Find those who are moving in the direction of purity and run with them. You'll have more strength with them than you ever will on your own.

LACK OF GROWTH OR DIRECTION

Purity only works if it is actively pursued. It's not the sort of thing that just happens. You won't find a married couple who never had sex while dating who will tell you, "Yeah, we didn't care about purity and meant to have sex before we got married. We just never got around to it." No, if they stayed pure, they applied conviction. But that conviction is not simply for the sake of purity. It's for something bigger.

Purity comes from wanting something bigger, something that requires purity. An aimless person who is not on a personal growth track has no reason to pursue purity, but someone who is on a positive mission will see purity as important to achieving their goal. The biggest goal that can be had is following God's mission for a person's life. Even if the specific call is still unclear, living God's way in the meantime is still a

---

9   1 Peter 5:8
10   2 Timothy 2:22, NASB95

worthy pursuit. But if a person is not growing and does not have a direction to move toward, purity may not stick. Find that greater sense of direction and understand why purity is important to achieving it.

> *"Accept the situation you are in and learn to be content about it."*

COVETOUSNESS AND LACK OF CONTENTMENT

There is a strange pattern found in the Bible. Whenever sexual impurity is mentioned, so is covetousness. This is because covetousness – the desire for other things to please us – is called idolatry.[11] When we want something that we cannot have, we are placing our own desire in the center of our lives as an object of worship. We idolize our own desires. Anyone who does that is bound to engage in hedonistic sexual passion. That's the tie-in.

But contentment is the antidote. Giving thanks was mentioned earlier. Accept the situation you are in and learn to be content about it. That does not mean you should not pursue your dreams of making things better, but you should be satisfied with where you are.

IT'S GOOD!

One other thing must still be said: Sex is good! Great even. When it is enjoyed within marriage, sex becomes a beautiful thing that leads to even more clarity. It's not a blissful frolic in the park. There are hurdles to overcome as a husband and wife get to know each other intimately, but even that develops character, clarity, and enjoyment. Consider that bright, enjoyable future, and give up any short-term pleasure that would dim your clarity now and enjoyment later.

---

11   See Ephesians 5:5 and Colossians 3:5

CHAPTER SIX

SPIRITUAL FLAGS

Do you have a favorite food? Maybe there's a dish that you cannot get enough of recently. It could be a stir fry or a gourmet taco, a new twist on a salad, or comfort food that both warms your bones and sticks to them. Imagine one of these favorite dishes and consider what it would taste like if you removed an ingredient. It wouldn't be the same without it. Many dishes go from average to amazing simply by including one ingredient.

Your life can take on new meaning and depth if you include spiritual growth. Spiritual attention will season every other dimension. Personal pursuits hold increased significance and direction; goals become sharper even as contentment grows; relationships extend to deeper levels and complexity. Yes, your relationships can take on a new character with attention to spiritual growth.

Many people cannot figure out why their relationships are stale and shallow. They languish because spiritual depth has been removed. It's the ingredient that pulls all the others together into one amazing dish. The mantra we hear these days does not necessarily discourage spiritual growth, but it does imply that we can find this key ingredient elsewhere. In fact, every advertisement that flashes before your eyes tacitly promises that ingredient. Every social media influencer on Tik Tok pretends to have the ingredient – maybe through social justice or travel destinations or weird feats. Streaming giants attempt to convince you that their content will make you content; if you are entertained by them, you will enjoy this ingredient. Universities and career readiness programs hold out the promise that your ultimate satisfaction can be found through their courses. Sports fanatics think they hold the key to what brings real vitality to life. Even burrito joints make you think paying $2.79 to add a small glob of guacamole will do the trick.

Everyone knows life needs an added ingredient to make everything really come together, to maximize the enjoyment of the good while appreciating every moment and person to the fullest. Go ahead and spring for the guac sometimes because nothing is inherently wrong with these things, but they cannot offer the spiritual growth we all need to make it in life. Some people go through life like cooks in a kitchen, continually adding a dash of this or that, never realizing that only God offers what they crave. If you want the added flavor profile of the spiritual dimension for this dish called life, take note of the spiritual flags in this chapter. They help us with the wholeness we long for, which God offers to us in His Word.[1]

---

[1] See James 1:4

🚩 **Red Flag:** They try to get something from you that they can only get from God

> *"How are you going to find wholeness from someone who isn't whole?"*

Just like in the pursuits mentioned above, many people seek wholeness where it cannot be found, including in relationships. This is silly on its face, though. You are incomplete and broken on your own. Do you think you landed someone who has it all together? She may seem amazing, but she's broken, too. He might look like the total package, but you'll notice the cracks if you examine him more closely. How are you going to find wholeness from someone who isn't whole? Sure, some of our oddities and gaps fill in just by being together, but this is not the same as the spiritual wholeness we seek. That only comes from God.

Some people find themselves so low on self-esteem that they constantly seek affirmation from others. This often comes in the form of false humility. If you find yourself dating a person like this, you'll always be drained for compliments and feel constrained to give affirmation. It seems cute to some initially, but when the relationship is based on you as the constant source of emotional wellness for another person, you'll get burned out eventually. You cannot be the constant source to prop up someone's emotional well-being.

There are two big problems with this red flag. The first is that, by seeking wholeness from a source other than God, a person has just short-circuited any spiritual growth and maturity that could come. The one place where they could find wholeness gets excluded. That's already unhealthy, but then the second problem is that YOU become the source of their wholeness. You are asked to fill God's shoes and give all the affirmation and personal healing and wholeness they need. However skilled, gifted, and patient you may be, this is a job that you cannot possibly fill.

God saw this problem with His people Israel long ago, and he sent a man named Jeremiah to call it out, declaring, "For My people have committed two evils: they have forsaken Me, the fountain of living waters, to hew for themselves cisterns, broken cisterns that can hold no water."[2] Turning away from God and then seeking new sources for what only God can give: does not end well. You are a broken cistern, just like your boyfriend or girlfriend. Don't be the source of someone else's wholeness. Instead, find someone who will walk with you to that "spring of living water."

There are four key needs that only God can meet: acceptance, security, purpose, and identity. Acceptance comes when people see themselves as made in God's image, crafted uniquely by their Creator with a specific personality and capacity for growth and engagement in the world. The Bible has this to say about people as God's creation: "For You formed my inward parts; You wove me in my mother's womb. I will give thanks to You, for I am fearfully and wonderfully made; wonderful are Your works, and my soul knows it very well."[3] People cannot find a way to accept themselves without finding acceptance first from God. Without it, they will never be comfortable with who they are and will continually seek affirmation from others as little bandages for their insecurities. They may also become upset at the smallest things because their egos are so fragile that anything unexpected is perceived as an offense.

---

2   Jeremiah 2:13, NASB95
3   Psalm 139:13-14, NASB95

Security also can only be truly met by God. You might have an alarm for your home or one of those doorbell cameras, but folks with security issues will fritter their lives away with worry, never trusting that God is the One who keeps us safe. Security allows risk. It enables adventure. It keeps people from playing it safe all the time. Have you ever tried to convince someone it was safe to fly on a plane or ride that rollercoaster or do something adventurous? If a person isn't convinced of security, there won't be any movement. You'll likely find them retreating into a bubble of safety – their own little comfort cocoon they've crafted for themselves, not as a place to occasionally recharge but as their only area of felt security. This keeps them from taking risks, growing, and finding purpose.

The people most willing to take risks are those who understand that God guards them. They don't seek danger for the sake of thrill, but they remain undaunted by perceived threats. God often works through danger and even tragedy to bring about His good purpose. When our security centers on the good God brings and on our ultimate security – the hope of eternal life through Jesus – minor insecurities in this life do not trouble us. We can agree with this verse in the Bible: "And we know that God causes all things to work together for good to those who love God, to those who are called according to His purpose."[4]

Without that call of purpose from God, people will either content themselves with a purposeless existence or seek out purpose from sources that cannot grant it. You cannot grant someone purpose, but you can affirm a person's understanding of purpose. You can help them discover purpose by going to the right Source, where security and acceptance are found as well.

---

[4] Romans 8:28, NASB95

> "No matter what you have done or what family background you have, you have value."

Our identity, however, gives us confidence in who we are. We learn in Genesis that we have been created in God's image.[5] King David later poetically described the amazing care God gave to fashion him – and, by extension, all of us – as a work of art while he was still in the womb.[6] No matter what you have done or what family background you have, you have value. You get your value from God because He alone declares it. Your sense of worth must be grounded in God, or you will constantly seek affirmation from whatever source you mistakenly believe will provide it. While your treatment of others should reflect the intrinsic, God-given value that each person has, you can never give a person that value. A person who craves value from you will suck you dry.

▶ Green Flag: You spur one another on and help guide each other toward God

Pointing each other toward the right Source for these needs is a bright spot in any relationship. Why do people elevate sex and get hung up on conflict? It's because they lack something bigger in their relationship to pursue. Without the green flags, people find the red ones. Green spiritual flags bring fulfillment in a relationship that helps prevent couples from unhealthy tendencies. This is a lot like someone trying to eat right. If good, healthy food options are readily available, it's much easier to avoid junk food. But if someone is hungry and a bag of chips is the only thing within reach, it'll be hard to eat just

---

5   See Genesis 1:27
6   See Psalm 139, especially verses 13-16.

one! Healthy practices replace unhealthy ones and bring double benefits to a relationship.

What are the other benefits of couples encouraging each other toward God?

First, they agree to conform to an outside standard. The guy encourages the girl to follow God, and the girl likewise encourages the guy. They don't say, "Conform to my expectations," which would be arbitrary and inconsistent. They hold a shared expectation to go in the same direction of spiritual growth. This means you both know where you're headed spiritually together. Imagine all the life problems that come (and they will); for every one of them, know that you can handle them together. Some people mess this up, wanting to push a different standard. *He wants me to be like his mother*, a woman realizes. *Three months ago, he couldn't stand her, but now he wants to be taken care of by me just the way she did for him as a boy.* He's flip-flopping with an arbitrary standard. Little expectations will exist, but they can be adjusted and must fit around the biggies. The biggies are the spiritual elements. A guy who understands this fact won't compare her to his mother but will instead encourage his lady toward caring for others the way God does. God's standard becomes the pattern to follow.

Second, they accept progress and setbacks. Because they are both on a journey, they understand that sometimes people move along faster or slower. Have you ever had someone who couldn't tolerate a whiff of failure? It's not okay to have disappointments or to fall short of expectations with people like that. They are either cyborgs, or they hold others to a standard of perfection that they themselves don't hold to. They often make excuses for themselves and blame others for their faults.

79

Do you want that in any relationship? When you see each other on a path of growth, forgiveness comes much easier. You can look at those failures and disappointments through the lens of growth. You can understand that it may be a bad day but that God is still helping you both grow to be more like Him.

You also understand your role in helping him or her toward something important. The marriage relationship – and the dating relationship before it – is largely about helping someone else grow closer to God. He can wake up and consider *how my interactions can encourage her relationship with God.* She can respond softly to his rude remark made from the point of stress, realizing that her response can help him get back on the right track. When you both see yourselves as playing a supporting role toward the other's growth, you find yourself aligning better with the purpose behind relationships in the first place. If you can find that rhythm, you're in a great spot!

But the best benefit – the cherry on top – is that you enjoy a much better relationship. It's smoother, more stable, and more fun. You realize that you are on the same team together and can work together. There are no trust issues that lead you toward selfishness to get what you can. You have someone to talk to and be open with, and you know you are both headed in the same direction.

Here's one way that couples screw this up: they date someone who doesn't share their purpose. This is definitely bad if that person does not follow God (see below), but it's also damaging if that person's pursuits don't align with your own. They date and then marry for looks or outward appearances but do not consider the life direction and goals a person has. A woman is working her way toward VP of Sales in some swanky company, and she dates someone who is passive and lacks ambition. Do you think he's going to understand you and spur you on toward your goals? Nope. Not going to happen. You'll feel like you're dragging him along like dead weight, and you'll be embarrassed because everyone else will see it, too. Then your pursuits will be separate from his. Is that what you wanted from your most intimate relationship? Or the man is ambitious and marries a girl who looks flashy but is shallow. That's going to show. She may seem like a ten, but he'll internally groan whenever she opens her mouth because there's no real thought behind it.

Find someone who engages on the same level in terms of ambition and passion and who is spiritually willing to work together with you toward a common goal.

> **Green Flag: You both love Jesus and are passionately pursuing Him**

So how do you find a person who is willing to spur you on? You find someone who already loves Jesus and is following Him. This is a pre-dating activity. Develop now the spiritual practices that you expect to be in place during your marriage. Get into the habits that you want to be present in both of your lives. Yes, this involves good habits with prayer, reading your Bible, studying God's Word with others, and going to church. If you want spiritual depth in your life and marriage one day, you must start now.

You also must refuse to date someone who is not already passionately pursuing Jesus. Promise yourself you won't do it. Tell a friend and ask the friend to help you keep to it. You've seen people get derailed by this (maybe you have in the past, too). He's growing spiritually, but then he meets this girl at

> *"... keep the discipline to love and pursue Jesus and never date someone who isn't already doing the same."*

work. She comes to church once or twice – goes along with it – but she holds no passion for Jesus. A girl will do the same thing when she meets a guy. "But I can help him follow Jesus." Ha! It won't happen. You have about a one in a thousand chance that he'll become as passionate about Jesus as you are. "Well, our relationship is one in a million," she replies.

If you compromise on this standard – if you decide to date someone who doesn't love Jesus, who doesn't passionately pursue Him – the damage is already done. You just don't know it yet. You have basically told God that you don't have enough faith in Him to bring along the right person at the right time. Instead, you need to take a shortcut because this is your only chance at love. You have also decided that your relationship with this person is more important than your relationship with Jesus, so you have already compromised on pursuing Him. And you've convinced yourself that you'll be the savior here? That job belongs to Jesus, and you just took it away.

No, the only thing that will do is to keep the discipline to love and pursue Jesus and never date someone who isn't already doing the same. If you compromise, you'll be the one dragged down. Do you need an example of this? There are plenty. Just look at the seats in the church that are filled once a month or once every other month. They are occupied by people who hold other pursuits. If you are okay with someone drifting from Jesus while dating, what do you think will happen in marriage? The façade of pseudo-commitment will disappear altogether, and you'll realize you have married someone who does not really follow Jesus.

How do you grow deeply with someone who does not have the same spiritual pursuits as you do? You cannot connect with him or her on the deepest, most intimate level there is. You'll find yourself compromising on spiritual goals just to keep the peace. And then the kids will come along. Without a shared commitment to raising them to follow Jesus, the kids will never have the spiritual depth you always dreamed for them. Separation from the ideals you once held will only increase over time. The Bible calls this being "bound together with unbelievers;"[7] some older translations render this as "unequally yoked," a term that refers to farm animals like oxen being connected by a heavy double harness – the yoke – and working together. They cannot do that if they hold different pursuits; if they seek different goals. The most extreme version of being unequally yoked is when a Christian marries a non-Christian, but this can also happen when you marry someone who is half-hearted in matters of faith.

FIND A STEEPLE

If you wanted to marry an athlete, would you join a chess club or a knitting group? Would you find a Lord of the Rings fan club to search for an athlete there? You *might* find your perfect, athletic soul mate at these places, but they aren't the most likely. If you wanted to find an athlete to marry, you might get a gym membership that you actually use and get involved in some of the fitness classes. You might get season tickets for a team or join a sports club. The point is that you put yourself in the best situation to find the sort of person you're looking for.

---

[7] 2 Corinthians 6:14, NASB95

To find someone who holds the same value for the spiritual flags, put yourself where people pursue Jesus. That's the church. There you can grow, and as you do, you'll find others doing the same. When you find people going the same direction – pursuing Jesus – you'll be more likely to come across the person to date and eventually marry. And even if you encounter that person somewhere else (like a chess club), you'll have an idea of what commitments to look for because you have seen them in other Christians and have been living them out yourself.

CHAPTER SEVEN

PERSONAL GROWTH FLAGS

Marriage can be a pressure cooker. It isn't for the faint of heart and can be difficult enough even for the well-equipped. Wading into the marital waters, then, without being fully ready, will apply more pressure than many relationships can bear. You really don't want to wind up married to someone who has not yet matured enough to handle marriage. Personal growth is all about becoming the person God intends you to be. These flags will help you spot who is and isn't ready for a committed relationship.

> **Red Flag:** When they are not okay with being single

Most young people still hope to enjoy marriage one day.[1] Singleness conveys many benefits, but most do not want to

---

[1] Yes, marriage per se is on the decline, but although some do not want to get married, they nevertheless desire a lifelong committed relationship with someone else. This is still an ideal of marriage and all that it represents.

85

stay single forever. This is okay, of course. It's natural. Most of us have a built-in desire to get married.

But singleness itself is a gift. Some enjoy it as a temporary gift until marriage, and others enjoy it all their lives, whether they expect to or not. But wait a second. Enjoy it? Singleness? Yes – what else do you do with a gift? People struggle with seeing singleness in this way, approaching it rather like a hurdle to overcome, a disease to recover from, a jail cell to escape. Ironically, single people enjoy more freedom than married people, but they don't realize it. If you live in a four-season climate zone, then you know that every summer, when the temperature is blast-furnace hot, and the humidity makes it hard to breathe, people go around saying, "I can't wait until winter." Then in the winter, when the frigid temps make the air feel like ice needles, and the wind somehow can blow straight through your bones, people start declaring, "I can't wait until summer." That's the fallen human condition: Whatever we have, we want the opposite.

And that's how it is with married people who miss their days of freedom and singleness and with single people who long for marriage. It's okay to reminisce and even long for these things, but they must be combined with contentment. Paul, the apostle, said that he had "learned to be content whatever the circumstances...[and] learned the secret of being content in any and every situation."[2] It is possible to learn to be content with your singleness, and it just may save you a boat load of heartache.

---

[2] See Philippians 4:11-12.

THE DANGER OF DISCONTENTMENT

Discontented people endanger themselves by trying to force the situation. Single people are so desperate to escape their prison of singleness that they rush into a relationship and tie the knot quickly. They find themselves a warm, willing body and walk down the aisle as quickly as possible. If you get yourself married at lightspeed, how many flags do you think you were able to pay attention to? You just rushed right past them all.

People can marry out of desperation slowly, too. They wind up in a long dating relationship with someone who isn't the right fit – there are some flag issues – but they never break it off for fear that they won't find anyone better or at all. They settle for a marriage partner.

Does marriage consume your thoughts? Do you find yourself on dating sites morning, noon, and night? Is it difficult to be happy for friends who get married because of the self-pity that comes? I don't know your situation, but please hear this warning: You are in danger of acting in desperation, which will bring even more pain.

People who marry out of desperation often commit a few errors that hurt themselves. First, they ignore warning signs. There's evidence that the person they've married is not ready for marriage. Maybe he shows signs of controlling or of being too passive, or she is love-bombing you to cover over her character flaws, and you're too desperate to see it. Pretending the warning signs aren't there doesn't make them go away!

Second, they compromise their standards. They are willing to give up important things just so they can get married. Maybe you used to say you wouldn't date a woman unless she was

> **"Marriage has become an idol."**

very involved in her faith, but now you're dating someone whose last time in church was with her grandma while in eleventh grade on Christmas Eve. Maybe you rightly determined to only date a guy who would respect your purity and treat you like you deserve, but then you reversed course and determined that sacrificing your purity was the only way to please a man enough to get married (In many cases, you just removed much of his incentive to get married!). Or you marry someone who has some major growing up to do, but you figure that can happen while married. But what if they don't grow up? What if she never cares about your faith? What if he's prone to infidelity? Our compromises sow the seeds of future suffering.

Third, they distort their vision. A desperate single person who once dreamed of a beautiful marriage with a wonderful spouse now craves an average marriage with any spouse. The very act of compromising standards compromises the picture of marriage, but people have obsessed about it so much that they don't realize how much their vision has shifted. Marriage used to symbolize a bright, stable future that leads to joy, but now it's little more than a relationship status that a person craves, forgetting what made it special. Marriage has become an idol.

WHAT TO PURSUE WHILE SINGLE

Don't exchange the glory of marriage for an idolatrous substitute. While you are single, you can pursue both personal growth and special endeavors in a way you will not be able to later. As you do, you'll find that God is preparing you for your future, whether that involves marriage or continued singleness.

While you may aspire to marriage, the goal is to be okay with singleness for as long as you are single. That contentment mentioned above can be elusive, but you can be content by focusing on some specific things while single.

YOUR RELATIONSHIP WITH GOD

The most important relationship to zero in on is your relationship with God. Learn to spend time with God and grow as you engage with the Bible and prayer. Pour your satisfaction into God and into knowing Him.

FAITH IN GOD'S PLAN

Remind yourself that you trust God's plan for your life. There are many twists and turns to life, and you never know what God has in store through even the smallest of avenues. If you focus on pursuing God and trust that His plan is best, you can rest confident without worrying.

PATIENCE

Some people have noted that God is never late but seldom early. God is patient, and following Him requires patience from us. It is easy to project manage your life and determine that you must get married by a certain age or stage of life, but God's timing may be different. This is the same God who promised to make a seventy-five-year-old childless man into a great nation and still waited twenty-five more years to give him the promised son! Trusting God's timing is an exercise in patience.

GRATITUDE

Exercising thankfulness will be a check to the times when feelings of self-pity attack. Count your blessings. Start naming all the good things in your life: family, friends, unexpected kindness, provision for your needs, employment – whatever you can think of. Think big and small. Without gratitude, your heart will drift, and your orbit will center more and more on yourself.

MAKE THE MOST OF THIS TIME

Many married people got married without realizing how tied down they would become. Your lives will intertwine in a way that limits your freedom. When you add kids later, this becomes an even bigger deal. While you're single, consider what you can enjoy and participate in. You can more easily travel, go on mission trips, spend time helping elderly relatives, or use your evenings and weekends to help others in need or spontaneously have fun. That's a gift that you won't have nearly as often in marriage.

While you're free without a spouse, don't tie yourself down in other ways. Some people get high-maintenance pets for companionship, but the schedule required by pets keeps them from the very spontaneity they could be enjoying. Pets are great, but consider waiting until you are already tied down to get a pet option that will significantly impact your schedule.

Amy was a young adult volunteering in her church's youth ministry. When the opportunity came to go on the high school mission trip to Taiwan, she enthusiastically signed up. All signs were a go for this great trip: her calendar was clear, she had time off from work, and the opportunity was fabulous. Yet something was wrong. Amy couldn't quite put her finger on it, but she sensed that God was telling her not to go on the mission trip. After talking with the youth pastor, she decided not to go to Taiwan but agreed to join the middle school group on a much smaller mission trip to another church in a neighboring state for some service projects. While on that trip, Amy met Jason, a volunteer with the other church. The two of them began a relationship that led to a happy marriage. Pursue the opportunities you have while single and wait for God's timing. Trust Him to bring the right person your way.

> *"While impressing seems important, progressing is far more valuable."*

▶ **Green Flag: You both value personal growth**

Do you know how a new relationship is filled with exciting changes for both the guy and the girl? She starts going to the gym more often and chooses her outfits more carefully. He wears a clean shirt. They both spend more energy crafting texts and reading into the other's posts. She mentions liking a certain flower and – Poof! – the very next day, a bouquet of them appears at her workplace. Yeah, all that doesn't last. You already know this, but after marriage, it all gets dialed *way* back. A guy doesn't have to impress a girl once he marries her because she's stuck with him. And folks may later say, "She really let herself go," because she stopped trying to impress him, too. This is not all bad. It just means that eventually, you both realize that neither of you is very impressive, but you are two people who love each other and are committed to each other.

While *impressing* seems important, *progressing* is far more valuable. To impress involves using your existing qualities, while to progress involves expanding your capabilities. Personal growth allows a relationship to reach new depths of complexity and enjoyment, bringing increased appreciation and respect for your partner.

But if only one of you grows personally, you will wind up mismatched, creating more distance between you. If you value personal growth, ensure that your future spouse is committed to it, too. This requires observation. Gauge growth over time and observe what positive changes you see. You want to notice progress in their growth and development. Look for deepening character and increasing maturity. Talk about a trait you are trying to improve; for example, share that you are working on being more patient or less quick-tempered. Open the topic of personal growth and look for engagement. If you do not see progress or even engagement, you may need to move on.

Personal growth ideally exists in matters beyond character, such as physical fitness, lifelong learning (formal or informal), career advancement, or family strengthening. People are designed to improve themselves over time. The personal growth process reflects what it means to be made in the image of God. Even Jesus underwent personal growth.[3] Some people do not have the desire to grow, or they plateau, deciding they have achieved a sufficient level in life. If you are married to such a person, your growth will be frustrated by the lack of growth you see in your spouse.

Some people see a lack of personal growth in an area and attempt to force the issue to more overtly ask for the growth they wish to see in someone. Let's say you convince your boyfriend to start running with you. He would otherwise have no desire to run, but he agrees because he cares about you.[4] His efforts will always follow yours. Unless he catches the running bug deep within his soul, you will find no initiative from

---
[3] See Luke 2:42 for one example.
[4] This is just an example. Unless your life revolves around running, don't break up with the poor guy just because he doesn't hit the track.

him, only responses to your pushing, prodding, and coaching. You're a runner, but he's not. He's willingly going along with you (for now), but you'll be pushing him to run every step of the way. You will likely get tired of it over time.

What if, instead of running, the issue was character related? How do you push someone externally for something that requires internal motivation?

You can't. It won't work.

Whatever you push for in him will always be the result of your own external prodding. You'll be running the whole show while he remains passive. Later, you will be perceived as a nag because you keep pushing for what you thought were shared values between you but are things that only you have ever cared about. His frustration with your nagging will be matched only by your disappointment in his lack of leadership.

While you cannot will into existence a commitment to personal growth, you can encourage it when you find it. You cannot nurture a plant that doesn't exist, but you can help even the smallest plant grow healthy and strong. Encourage what is there and look for growth. Support small expressions of growth and see how you can help. She may want to get a new job certification, and you offer to help her study. Maybe she mentions wanting to pray more, so you both take turns praying together each night. When you find ways to share growth, your relationship will better reflect the sacrificial love of marriage – giving of yourself to help make the other better.[5]

---

5   See Ephesians 5:25-28, where husbands in particular are to show the sacrificial love of Jesus, who gave Himself up to make His bride – the Church – better.

HOW'S YOUR GROWTH?

If you are on the lookout for someone who is personally ready to handle marriage, expect that future soulmate to be wise enough to be searching for the same readiness in you. What areas of your life are you intentionally improving? It could be better financial habits, a character issue to correct, or more regular involvement in a Bible study. A person who values growth and finds you already growing will be attracted to you, but if you aren't already growing, that person will likely keep looking for the right person for the green flag. Take steps today to begin growing if this is not yet a habit for you.

CHAPTER EIGHT

SOCIAL FLAGS

Oh, the thrill of being alone together! To gaze into each other's eyes, captivated in wonder and filled with warm "tingles" that course through you. If you have ever experienced this, then you know it doesn't last. Honestly, would you want to look at *yourself* that long? Those raw feelings, as nice as they are, cannot last. They were never meant to.

Any durable romantic relationship must exist within social connections. We are, after all, social creatures who need several relationships with others. Your relationship with your spouse will be the most intimate earthly relationship you have, and during the dating process, you should, as you discover that this person would make a good spouse, move from less relational intimacy to more. The social relationships that you have, both individually and as a couple, are themselves indicators – flags – of the maturity you have and the compatibility[1] you share.

---

[1] This compatibility refers to personal goals, spiritual habits, and career plans rather than the mystical horoscope-style compatibility often discussed in our culture.

Two red flags and one green flag can be found in the social relationships you have that hold clues about your readiness for marriage together.

🚩 **Red Flag: When others don't celebrate the relationship**

This first flag is a big warning sign that many disregard to their peril. Maybe you have seen this play out. Perhaps you have been the one who didn't celebrate your friend's relationship. Your friend comes in so enamored with her new boyfriend. You put up with the too-giddy laughter and slightly nauseating playfulness as you try to get to know this new person, but you realize something is off. Maybe you ask some get-to-know-you questions that he doesn't really answer or give evasive responses. Maybe your friend keeps jumping in to answer for him, and you find that he is ignoring you and her other friends altogether.

Or your friend comes with his new girlfriend, and you can see clearly that she is manipulating him, using "that tone" to get him to do whatever she wants. The veneer is just a little too obvious. You may even ask him questions and find that she jumps in to answer for him with responses that don't fit your friend. You can easily understand the saying that love is blind – and foolish and a bit stupid.

Admit to yourself now that when you get enamored with your new boo, you will be wearing blinders for a little while. You will miss things your friends see almost immediately because you are so smitten that you can only see all the good traits. You even explain away the trouble signs and find ways to call them good. Your friends have another perspective.

They know you and care about you. If they don't celebrate the relationship, you should pay attention.

The Book of Proverbs says a lot about listening to the good advice of others:

> *"The way of a fool is right in his own eyes, but a wise man is he who listens to counsel."*[2]

> *"He who trusts in his own heart is a fool, but he who walks wisely will be delivered."*[3]

> *"Faithful are the wounds of a friend, but deceitful are the kisses of an enemy."*[4]

> *"A friend loves at all times, and a brother is born for adversity."*[5]

That's just a sample. Over and over, God advises His people to listen to good advice from trusted people. That does assume you have wise friends. "He who walks with wise men will be wise, but the companion of fools will suffer harm."[6] Ensure you surround yourself with people who love God, care about you, and are maturing themselves. If your friends are all over the map, living out of control, they likely won't notice or care that something is off about your new boyfriend or girlfriend. Assuming you have good friends, though, listen to them!

Somehow people think their friends have good advice in all cases except when they do not celebrate a romantic relationship. All sorts of claims begin to fly around, threatening to destroy the friendship just because a friend shared misgivings about

---

2 Proverbs 12:15, NASB95
3 Proverbs 28:26, NASB95
4 Proverbs 27:6, NASB95
5 Proverbs 17:17, NASB95
6 Proverbs 13:20, NASB95

that hunk you started lugging around with you. "She's jealous." "They're haters." Suddenly you are far wiser than your friend when just last week you couldn't make avocado toast without her advice. Please! There's a warning in Galatians: "For if anyone thinks he is something when he is nothing, he deceives himself."[7] Don't deceive yourself by thinking you now have it all together. Your friends are not trying to mess up something good. They're trying to prevent you from getting clobbered by a relationship with serious red flags.

People who don't listen to their friends in this will often isolate themselves from their boyfriend or girlfriend. Although their friends see the red flags, people avoid their friends out of desperation to ignore the warning signs that are there. Isolation will not keep you from danger. It's like being in a little canoe on a river with people on the shoreline shouting that you're headed toward a huge waterfall, and you stick your earbuds in and crank the tunes to "ignore the haters." This won't end well.

Because of how awkward speaking up can be, sometimes your friends will keep silent, but they will give indicators that they can't celebrate the relationship. They'll start acting a little funny when you bring your boyfriend or girlfriend around. You'll see a certain expression. It's like the expression people give when someone tells an inappropriate joke. It's kind of funny, but they know they shouldn't laugh, so instead, they give an awkward smile of embarrassment while looking away. That's the same kind of expression your shy friends will give when you bring your love interest around. They don't want to come out and say this person is bad for you, so they give

---

[7] Galatians 6:3 NASB95

off these awkward expressions as flares, hoping you pick up on the problem.

That's why you should ask your friends what they think. Check in after a month, three months, or six months to ask about what they see – good or bad – and listen. Hopefully, your friends will be willing to share their concerns if they have them. If this person is right for you, then your relationship is helping you become better, and your friends should see that positive growth.

This goes for family, too. Your dad, mom, brothers, sisters, and even Aunt Cynthia (but maybe not your Uncle Stu) are the people who know you best. Add to that list pastors, coworkers, Bible study members, and others who care about you and can see things about the relationship more clearly than you can.

When you bring your girlfriend to meet friends and family, it's an interview! She shouldn't feel put on the spot or as though she is being interrogated. She should understand that these people who care about you are watching her interactions with you – and them – to determine whether she is a good fit for you or not.

If she is a good fit, you will notice good relationships forming between her and them. There will be joking, laughter, and sharing things of significance. There will likely even be the occasional social outing that doesn't include you because good relationships are forming between her and people who not only care about you but also have begun to care about her. Ensure that others can celebrate the relationship, or there will be problems.

> **Red Flag:** They have more opposite-sex friends than same-sex friends

A person's closest friends ought to be of the same sex. For some of you, that's controversial. Women whose friends are almost all males might say they are not into the drama that comes from female relationships, and men whose friends are almost all females might say they are tired of the shallow immaturity of other guys.[8] You may have had these sorts of experiences or have other reasons for mostly opposite-sex relationships, but this is not healthy.

You can't paint with a broad brush and say that all members of your sex – except you, somehow – have a certain character deficiency that only the opposite sex remedies. That's just an excuse to cover up something else. When all your friends are of the opposite sex, something is wrong.

God designed men to build friendships with other men and women to build friendships with other women. They form close bonds and can have deep conversations about things that matter. When a marriage comes, these friendships can stay in place and take on a new character that won't hinder the marriage.

What happens on the flip side? Let's say you're a guy who marries a woman whose four closest friends are other men. You know that she will want to talk to her friends to sort out issues that arise in your marriage – all women do (men, too). Do you really want her sharing this or that marriage issue with other guys?

---

8   Most likely, the guy is infatuated with at least one of these ladies.

WATCH THE FLAGS

If you are a guy and don't enjoy having conversations with other dudes, something is wrong. I don't mean every dude. Some guys are gearheads who love talking about cars. If you aren't into cars, that may not be the strongest relationship. But guys need other guys to help each other stay sharp and focused on the right things, just as ladies need other ladies.[9]

> *"Find friends who are moving in the same direction you are spiritually."*

Consider whether this flag is yours to wave. It's okay to have some opposite-sex friendships, but they should not be your closest ones. Later, when you get into a dating relationship, these friendships will need to change. A guy can't have a night out with his lady friends when he has a girlfriend.

It could be that you have had trouble finding same-sex friendships because you are looking in the wrong spot. Find friends who are moving in the same direction you are spiritually. Look for them in a Bible study. Or look for friends whose positive goals are similar to yours. Then be friendly and see what relationships form.

But it could also be that you struggle with something in your life that prevents connection with friends of the same sex. Maybe you were hurt by someone in the past in a way that makes these friendships difficult. If you believe these relationships are difficult for you, you would be wise to seek counseling to help uncover an underlying issue.

▶ Green Flag: You have healthy lifelong friends

Given the verses mentioned earlier about friendship and wise counsel, you can be sure that God wants each one of us

---

9   See Proverbs 27:17, which explains same-sex friendships for keeping each other sharp.

to have good friends. These companions give input into our lives and are reliable supports to us. The giant sequoia redwood tree has a shallow root system that does not support the tree's great height. It stays upright and strong because those roots interconnect with those of other sequoias. Quality friendships are much the same, with each friend providing support to the others to keep them all upright.

A dating relationship relies on quality friendships, too. Other friends are a must for a couple's own relational health. Don't be the only friend of your boyfriend or girlfriend. You'll be miserable. You'll find yourself saddled with a job you were never meant to handle. Friends are supposed to be an outlet that brings outside opportunities and perspectives that, by definition, cannot be handled within a couple's relationship.

If the person you date has no friends (of the same sex, see the flag above), then there is a problem. There should be three to five close friends who know him and have maintained a relationship with him going back years. If he tells you some sob story about his friends turning on him in middle school and then high school and then three months ago, that's a big red flag waving in your face. He cannot keep close friends for some reason.

But if your boyfriend or girlfriend does have those friends, they are a great resource to you! Get to know them. Befriend them. If they are good friends, they will be interviewing you, but you should interview them, too. Learn more about your boyfriend or girlfriend. It's actually a great date idea: Go out together along with these friends and ask them for information.

You should be concerned if each friend is shallow, immature, or full of turmoil in life. Sure, one or two friends may be rough around the edges. You can't judge him based on a couple of problems his friends have. But if all the friends have big character issues, then it's a sign that he does, too. If all her friends seem shallow and out of touch with reality, she may also be.

People can sometimes get weird about their friends, as though they are the enemy. He had his friends before you, and he still wants to spend a lot of time with you. The same goes for her. Friends are allies. You can get to know her better by getting to know her friends. And if the friends like you-- well, you'll be in a great spot.

BE FRIENDLY

Your boyfriend or girlfriend's relationships are very important to them, so they should be important to you. The best way to nurture your relationship is to be friendly toward family members, friends, and coworkers. They will want to know you better, just as you will want to get to know them. This is all good because it reflects care for the relationship. They are watching out for the flags just as you are.

Encourage those friendships and know that they help your relationship thrive. Help support the friends, too, as an extension of your care for their friend. When you do, they will also support you. Don't ignore the social flags, for they represent some of the strongest bonds that make or break a great relationship.

CHAPTER NINE

CONFLICT FLAGS

Cue the fireworks because here comes conflict! Yes, no matter how healthy the relationship – how many green flag zones you've navigated while avoiding the red flags – there will be conflict. Conflict is what happens when you don't agree on something you deem too important to ignore. When it is handled well, the outcome is a beautiful thing. But it isn't often handled well, is it?

Done right, conflict can grow a relationship. Instead of presenting a barrier, conflict presents an opportunity. Disagreements expose us to alternate points of view, expanding our horizons if we'll let them. They can give you a window into the soul of your soulmate while providing you both an opportunity to express the fruit of the Spirit.[1]

---

1   See an explanation of the Fruit of the Spirit in chapter one on character flags.

But this assumes you both can handle conflict in a healthy way. Before getting to that, consider the red and green flags of conflict.

🚩 Red Flag: When they are conflict imploders or exploders

Conflict by design is meant to be dealt with. There's an issue and two adults who love each other both work together on a solution. But what if one party won't work on a solution? Conflict by nature makes us uncomfortable because it forces us to confront our own rough edges. God uses conflict to smooth us out, much like river rocks that have tumbled among each other for years. Because it's uncomfortable, though, some people find ways to avoid conflict. For them, conflict is more than uncomfortable; it's unbearable, and they employ techniques to escape a disagreement rather than deal with it.

Some people are conflict imploders. They shut down when there is a disagreement. You try to work with them toward a solution but find yourself alone. There are many ways to shut down. People will go silent and not engage in discussion, or they will leave, physically removing themselves from any attempt to work through something. This may also include sarcastic, self-deprecating remarks as a person leaves the room. Do you know the scenario where in an argument, the wife says, "I'm going to my mother's house"? That's an implosion. It's an attempt to leave rather than solve a problem.

Imploders practice avoidance techniques and will not meaningfully engage in attempts to resolve the issue. They may hear you out but contribute nothing, giving no response and leaving you wondering what they are even thinking. Feeling like you are talking to a mannequin is one sign that you have an imploder. The same avoidance can also be expressed by making a comment and leaving the room. "I must be the worst person on earth!" Exit stage right.

The exploders are the opposite. They'll turn on you as soon as you broach a subject that exposes a fault. Because of immaturity and fear of vulnerability, the exploder moves into self-defense, attacking the perceived threat: you. He may belittle you and your concerns. She may attempt to turn the tables and point out your faults. The exploder may storm off as well, but not before lobbing a few shots your way, whether insults or complaints.

> "... working through the conflict – the act itself – is an exercise in self-improvement."

Exploders can be smooth, too. Some are able to remain perfectly calm while refusing to accept blame and somehow pinning it all on you. When they really explode, you can easily know they have a problem with conflict, but when they keep it level, it becomes more difficult to see through the subtlety that they refuse to accept responsibility.

Don't write off your conflict imploders or exploders immediately. Many of the red flags in this book are hard stops. That's for good reason. Someone is not yet mature enough to handle a relationship. While this may also be true in the area of conflict, working through the conflict – the act itself – is an exercise in self-improvement. There are ways that you may be able to encourage someone with implosion or explosion tendencies to engage in the conflict resolution process.

That's the goal in a healthy relationship, in a marriage. You want to enable the other's improvement. If you both value personal growth (see chapter seven), then you both can help each other navigate conflict in a way that leads to growth.

BE A CONFLICT RESOLVER

When working through conflict, there are at least two levels of activity: the conflict itself and the process of resolving it. Imploders and exploders short circuit the resolution process, but part of your job is to help walk through the process. When you set the stage for success, you will enjoy better results. How can you do this? Consider these practical steps for situations when you confront someone about an issue:[2]

Step one: Consider the conflict. Although your first inclination might be to address conflict head-on, you will avoid making a situation worse if you are willing to stop and consider the issue. Consider your motivation. A Christian should desire to glorify God through conflict.[3] God is the great Reconciler who restored our relationship with Himself through the death and resurrection of Jesus. We also must seek reconciliation, which glorifies God.

Consider your understanding of the conflict. Can you state it succinctly and refer to behavior that you have observed? Try to see the issue through the other person's eyes and ponder what interests may be involved. Think through what outcome you would like. What reasonable solution will you seek?

Then consider your own contribution to the conflict. This is called getting the log out of your own eye. It comes from these words that Jesus spoke:

Why do you look at the speck that is in your brother's eye but does not notice the log that is in your own eye? Or how can

---

[2] Many of the following principles come from *The Peacemaker: A Biblical Guide to Resolving Personal Conflict,* by Ken Sande (Baker Books, 2nd ed. 1997).
[3] Bringing glory to God is the Christian's job in everything. See 1 Corinthians 10:31.

you say to your brother, "Let me take the speck out of your eye," and behold, the log is in your own eye? You hypocrite, first take the log out of your own eye, and then you will see clearly to take the speck out of your brother's eye.[4]

Get the log out of your own eye by taking responsibility for any role you have played in this process. If you see fault in yourself, take responsibility for that and be ready to share how you are willing to change.

Finally, consider whether the offense is minor. Don't sweat the small stuff! We read in Proverbs, "A man's discretion makes him slow to anger, and it is his glory to overlook a transgression."[5] In relationships, there is often an underlying problem that blows up because of a very small offense. Overlook these small offenses and instead only confront the problems that cannot be overlooked.

Step two: Seek resolution. Consider the best environment to bring up the problem. Obviously, texting her in the middle of her busy workday (or worse, showing up at work to talk about it) is going to be a bad idea, just as bringing it up in front of others would be. Within the right setting, state the issue clearly and in love. Mention any responsibility you bear in the situation.

Patiently wait for a response following a confrontation. You may be able to talk through the issue then and there, but that may not happen. Those with imploder tendencies often need time to digest what you've said. This is part of learning how someone else ticks and working that into the rhythm of your relationship. You may even need to create the space. "I noticed X, and it bothered me. Could we talk about that tonight or

---

4   Matthew 7:3-5, NASB95
5   Proverbs 19:11, NASB95

> *"... try to hear the problem before you respond..."*

tomorrow?" If you are willing to wait, you'll often find that the person has truly given careful consideration to what you said and is ready to make necessary changes.

Sometimes you are on the receiving end but haven't been given the courtesy of the steps above. That can be infuriating, especially if you are a recovering imploder or exploder. Since one layer of conflict is the process of resolving it, try to guide that process. If you are blindsided by a hasty claim that "you *always* do...," don't take the bait by starting to argue. Just apply the brakes. Ask for ten minutes to wait and think before you come together and talk about the problem. Then don't use your time to scroll your phone or call a friend to complain. Use it instead to consider and pray about the issue, and create a plan to discuss the issue in a level-headed way. When you come together, just try to hear the problem before you respond and ask for more time if you need it.

Step three: Make confession the right way. Whether you are confronted or are confronting conflict, you will often find that you have wronged another person. When this happens, don't duck responsibility with excuses or a half-hearted confession. Own up to your fault the right way. These are the *Seven A's of Confession:*[6]

- ▶ Address everyone involved. Anyone who was directly impacted should be included.

- ▶ Avoid *if*, *but*, and *maybe*. You have heard non-apologies before. They happen when someone says,

---
[6] The *Seven A's of Confession* come from Ken Sande's book *Peacemaker*

"I'm sorry *IF* you were offended, *BUT*...." It does not help.

▶ Admit specifically to what you did. Clearly state what it was instead of speaking generically.

▶ Apologize by expressing sorrow for the way you affected someone. Show that you have thought about the impact of your actions on others.

▶ Accept the consequences. Trust may need to be rebuilt, or restitution may need to be made. Be willing to take responsibility for that.

▶ Alter your behavior. Commit to changing harmful habits that led to the problem. This commitment will glorify God and go a long way toward reconciliation.

▶ Ask for forgiveness. Your request will give someone the opportunity to model forgiveness, which will bring healing for both of you and

Remember, your goal is to work through conflict together because you are both on the same team. If you can work through conflict like this, it is a great sign for your relationship. If not – if you are dealing with a true conflict imploder or exploder – then you will find yourself on the rotten end of every conflict.

▶ **Green Flag: There is grace and forgiveness in your relationship**

The resolution of conflict does not simply come because one party recognizes fault in some area; it comes because both parties are seeking a peace-filled resolution. Not all conflict comes when someone is at fault, per se. Sometimes there are communication breakdowns or things people just don't realize bother someone else, though they aren't wrong. Part of learning to understand each other involves communicating about expectations and differences that are the product not of improper behavior but of separate norms. When one of you has done something wrong, however – maybe he thought it would be funny to make fun of you in front of others – part of resolving the conflict means the other must extend grace and forgiveness.

Problems cannot be resolved unless you both want to resolve them. Sometimes we develop a victim attitude. We believe that the offense someone causes gives us license to be upset. Instead of helping to solve the problem, we flash our licenses and act upset, going around with a chip on our shoulders. Instead of getting over a hurt, we dwell on it and nurse it into a grudge. This happens in varying degrees to all of us, and maturity involves remembering the goal of conflict is resolution. To accomplish that, however, the offended person must give up the right to be upset.

If you find yourself in a relationship with someone who keeps a grudge, beware! Expect to spend many hours in the doghouse as penance for whatever small thing you did to make her upset this time. It won't simply be what you did this time that is the problem because she will remember the time before that – and before that, plus that thing you did at the New Year's Eve party three years ago – and hold you accountable for each little thing you've done. Or he will list all your faults completely unrelated to the offense you've caused him because, in his unforgiveness, he wants to include every unpleasant aspect of your character back at you. Conflict can never be resolved like this.

Avoid this situation by asking about prior relationships. This is important as you consider whether marriage is a possibility. Learning about these relationships helps you see signs not only of growth and maturity but also grace and forgiveness. If he describes four relationships, and in each one, his girlfriend turned out to be a psychopathic and cruel weirdo, what do you think is going to happen in your relationship? He will eventually find the same fault in you. Either he somehow is attracted to girls about to go crazy, which would be bad for you, or he has no clue how to take responsibility in conflict and grow as a person. If you aren't psychopathic and cruel, go with the second option. It also means that, if true, he has poor judgment. He somehow decided to get into multiple relationships with some real whackos without seeing any warning signs. The warning sign is for you: There is no green flag of grace and forgiveness here.

If that green flag is present, you will hear a balanced description of a relationship, where he describes some of his own faults along with hers. Or, instead of demonizing past boyfriends, she explains how she came to recognize that they cared about different things and discovered they were not a good match for each other. If she did date a crazy guy, there should still be some sense of personal responsibility for not handling the conflict well or not seeing warning signs. If what you hear is one big dump of victimhood about what he did, you may be accused of the same thing before long.

Grace and forgiveness are both terms we get from the Bible. God places high value on each of these. He expects His followers to model both traits, which is another reason why the church would be a great place to find someone to date.[7] Consider the conflict that God had with humanity and how He dealt with it. Because we sinned against Him, He was the offended party, and we were one hundred percent at fault. Yet God bent over backward to resolve this conflict. He came to earth and took the consequences for our actions on Himself by dying on the cross. That act of grace was followed by full forgiveness to any of us who place our faith in Jesus. If God were describing His relationship with humanity, He wouldn't have to admit to any blame. It was all our fault. But God took our blame on Himself, so eager He was to resolve the conflict of sin.

The Bible tells followers of Jesus, "Be kind and compassionate to one another, forgiving each other, just as in Christ God forgave you."[8] The forgiveness we have experienced must be extended to others if we truly follow the example of Jesus. It's a distinctive trait of Christians who have experienced forgiveness in full measure from God.

Showing grace involves overlooking an offense to appreciate the full value that a person has and, in conflict, extending yourself to find its resolution. That's a costly endeavor sometimes because we must choose to see peace rather than nurse a grudge. Showing forgiveness fully releases an offense

---

[7] It's funny how this keeps coming up, isn't it? See the spiritual flags in chapter six to learn more.
[8] Ephesians 4:32, NIV

so that it is no longer counted as even existing. When both people model this in a relationship, there is true strength that mirrors the core of God's own heart toward all of us.

GIVING COMPLETELY

Have you ever considered the fact that the word *give* is part of *forgive*? How ironic that the one who has been wronged has the job of giving! When we ask forgiveness of someone, we are essentially saying, "I did something wrong to you, and now I am asking you to give me something." Traced back to its roots, *forgive* means to give completely or fully.

> *"Showing forgiveness fully releases an offense so that it is no longer counted as even existing."*

Any relationship with forgiveness finds both parties willing to fully give of themselves for the other. They don't try to win every fight. They have redefined what it means to win. Winning is peace. Winning is forgiveness. Winning is restoration. The big win is that two imperfect people can be comfortable with each other, knowing that future hurts and screw-ups will come but that they can be handled, too. In this, two imperfect people put on dazzling display the good news of what God offers for all of us.

Cue the fireworks because conflict can lead to a great cause for celebration!

CONCLUSION

Now that you know the flags – the red and the green – what will you do? How will you respond to the principles you've read about? Remember, you are responsible for what you now know, but you have also been empowered, armed with new information to navigate both the dating world and life in general, making you better prepared for marriage with the right spouse God brings your way.

"A prudent man sees evil and hides himself; the naive proceed and pay the penalty."[1] Do you remember that verse? You are better able to see and avoid danger while also seeing and embracing good opportunities, chances to grow, improve yourself, and develop positive relationships.

So how can you best act on the flags? Maybe you read through and felt that you are doing great in nearly all of them, or maybe you came out thinking your life is a train wreck. More likely,

---

[1] Proverbs 27:12, NASB95

you find yourself somewhere between those two extremes. Here are three steps you can take to get started.

1. PICK TWO

No one can apply the principles of all the flags at once, but applying two of them is manageable. Identify a flag or two that you want to work on. Mark it in the book if you want to. Each one has an element for you to apply to yourself – to your own habits, thinking, and awareness. While you're looking, make a note of other flags you'd like to apply personally later.

Then make a different mark for flags that you've missed in others – perhaps a green flag was absent in someone you dated, or a red flag was present. Those flags may be areas for you to be more vigilant about in the future.

If you really want to get extreme, ask a friend to read the book and identify a flag for you to improve on.

2. START A NEW HABIT

As you begin to apply the principles of one or two flags, choose to start one habit that will help you move in the right direction. That habit could simply involve waking up thirty minutes earlier to start your day positively (or giving yourself a bedtime). You might decide to detox from social media or have two phone-free hours during the day. Reading your Bible for a few minutes a day and then considering how to apply what you read is a great habit if you haven't formed it yet. You could also get your spending under control with a budget.

The goal is to begin a habit that will create some space in your life to develop the things that matter most. Good habits make for a more well-ordered life; they go hand in hand with applying the flags.

3. FIND A CHURCH

Here's the truth: These flags don't really work on the individual level. They work best in a community of like-minded people. All the principles in this book either come straight from the Bible or tie in with its truth, so a church is a great place to start. You've read in several chapters about the importance of getting involved in a church, so find a church that cares about God's Word and be there regularly. Attend the weekly worship service.

If you already do that, then find a regular small group Bible study and join it. Many churches have Bible studies for singles, which means you can connect with others who are trying to grow just as you are. In the Bible, Paul gave this advice to young Timothy: "Now flee from youthful lusts and pursue righteousness, faith, love, and peace, with those who call on the Lord from a pure heart."[2]

"Along with those...." For the purposes of this book, we could rephrase that verse to say, "Flee the red flags and pursue the green ones, along with those who call on the Lord out of a pure heart." Find some people who are trying to order their lives the same way you are. You can all help motivate each other to keep pursuing what leads to vitality, and you can encourage each other when that pursuit becomes difficult.

That's why you must get involved in a church. It makes applying these important principles infinitely easier.

Finally, you are either not currently dating someone, or you have a boyfriend or girlfriend.[3] If you're flying solo right now, then follow the steps above on your own. If you are dating

---

[2] 2 Timothy 2:22, NASB95. This verse was also mentioned in chapter five.
[3] At least that's whom this book is primarily intended for. However, if you are married, consider going through this book with your spouse. It may be a great way to improve your relationship.

someone, then determine whether you should end that relationship or include that boyfriend or girlfriend in these next steps you'll take. If you cannot get them to read this book or apply what is in it, then that's a bonus red flag for you. If you care about following the advice on these pages, but they have no interest in it, that will lead to problems.

You've got this.

Because of the power of God, you've got this.

Because of those who have gone before you, you've got this.

Because of your capacity for change, you've got this.

Because of others who are actively doing the same thing, you've got this.

Because mistakes are just opportunities to start again, you've got this.

You've got this.

11 Red Flags

- ▶ When their character is not what attracts you to them
- ▶ When you expect marriage to fix the person
- ▶ They love bomb you
- ▶ You don't feel safe, and you change who you are to fit them
- ▶ They start dating you without getting over their ex
- ▶ When you do anything else
- ▶ They try to get something from you that they can only get from God
- ▶ When they are not okay with being single
- ▶ When others don't celebrate the relationship
- ▶ They have more opposite-sex friends than same-sex friends
- ▶ When they are conflict imploders or exploders

12 *Green Flags*

- You both exhibit the Fruit of the Spirit

- You can confidently show up as your authentic self

- You both understand that marriage involves selflessness

- You're both aware of the five buckets, and you're on your way to getting them refilled

- You talk for hours without knowing the time has passed

- You care about what you can give more than about what you can get

- You both realize purity leads to clarity and strive to remain pure

- You spur one another on and help guide each other toward God

- You both love Jesus and are passionately pursuing Him

- You both value personal growth

- You have healthy lifelong friends

- There is grace and forgiveness in your relationship